Intelligence on the Economic Collapse of Japan in 1945

Shannon McCune

UNIVERSITY
PRESS OF
AMERICA

Lanham • New York • London

University Press of America,® Inc.

4720 Boston Way
Lanham, MD 20706

3 Henrietta Street
London WC2E 8LU England

Printed in the United States of America

British Cataloging in Publication Information Available

Library of Congress Cataloging-in-Publication Data

McCune, Shannon Boyd–Bailey, 1913–
Intelligence on the economic collapse of Japan in 1945 /
Shannon McCune.
p. cm.
Includes bibliographical references.
1. Japan—Economic conditions—1918–1945. 2. World War, 1939–
1945—Military intelligence—Japan. I. Title.
HC462.8.M395 1989 330.952'033—dc20 89–16677 CIP

ISBN 0–8191–7560–9 (alk. paper)

The paper used in this publication meets the minimum requirements of American National Standard for Information Sciences—Permanence of Paper for Printed Library Materials, ANSI Z39.48–1984. ♾

With Thanks to my Colleagues in

The Economic Intelligence Section of the General Staff Intelligence, GHQ, India

The China Mission of the Foreign Economic Administration, Chungking, China

The Joint Intelligence Staff of the Joint Chiefs of Staff, Washington

The Men's Lunch Group of the United Church of Gainesville, and

The American Civilization Seminar of the University of Florida, Gainesville

TABLE OF CONTENTS

PREFACE

Economic intelligence on Japan was disseminated in the last months of World War II through Special Articles and Notes in the Weekly Summary of the Joint Intelligence Committee of the Joint Chiefs of Staff in Washington. The editing and writing of this economic intelligence was my responsibility as the Foreign Economic Administration's representative on the Joint Intelligence Staff. The Weekly Summary has been declassified, so that these materials are now available. They give a measured and contemporary view of Japan's economic collapse as it was going on in 1945.

For centuries Korean scholars in their retirement years have made collections of their writings. These collections, or chip, are useful for giving a sense of the times and events in the lives of these scholars. This collection of materials on the economy of Japan from the Weekly Summary of the spring and summer of 1945 are assembled and commented upon in this book, my chip of 1945.

Many people have assisted me in this project. I am thankful to William G. Lewis and his colleagues in the Military Field Branch of the Military Archives Division of the National Archives in Suitland, Maryland for arranging access to the Weekly Summary. I xeroxed parts of the issues published in 1945 and worked with these copies. During the summer of 1988, I read widely in the field of intelligence and the Pacific War in the excellent library of the Royal Military College in Kingston, Ontario.

In the fall of 1988 at the University of Florida I read a preliminary paper on the subject of economic intelligence at the American Civilization Seminar. I appreciated the comments of my colleagues in the Seminar and of other faculty members, particularly those of Yasushi Toda of the Department of Economics. My wife has helped greatly in editing materials and in encouraging me to prepare this chip. My son, Blair McCune, has been very supportive.

Shannon McCune

CHAPTER I

ECONOMIC INTELLIGENCE

The collection, analysis, dissemination and exploitation of economic intelligence have been carried on for many centuries. For example, in the Bible are stories of Israelites and others who as they spied out the land counted the sheep and the goats of their adversaries. The ruling kings and powers of Europe had their spies and advisors who sought to measure the economic strengths and weaknesses of their friends and enemies. Often, large European banking houses, the multi-national corporations of their days, gathered and used economic intelligence. Despite this long history there is relatively little literature on economic intelligence in the mass of material existing on intelligence and espionage activities.[1]

During World War I there was an economic intelligence section within military intelligence in the Department of the Army. This section was headed in 1918 by John Foster Dulles, who many years later served as Secretary of State.[2] In 1917 and 1918, though not confined to economic intelligence, the "Inquiry" had its headquarters at the American Geographical Society in New York and collected, analyzed and mapped economic intelligence on Europe.[3] This material was used by the American delegates to the Peace Conference at Versailles.

During World War II the British Ministry of Economic Warfare (MEW) and the American Board of Economic Warfare (BEW) were active in collecting, analyzing and disseminating economic intelligence. They exploited this material for their activities in economic warfare. They cooperated in their intelligence activities and made this economic intelligence available to governmental agencies, particularly to their respective Armed Forces.

During the early years of World War II an Office of Special Operations (SOE) was attached to the British Ministry of Economic Warfare.[4] This organization was involved in covert operations and had very little to do with economic intelligence or economic warfare. There are some interesting accounts of SOE activities in Europe where they had some notable successes. They used the cover of the British Ministry of Economic Warfare in setting up SOE offices in India. Thus, when the Ministry wished to establish an office for economic intelligence in India, their name was already being used. As a consequence, the "legitimate" MEW intelligence activity became the Economic Intelligence Section (EIS) of the General Staff, Intelligence, India (GSII) of the General

Headquarters in India (GHQ, India). When intelligence officers from the American Board of Economic Warfare, such as myself, went to India in 1943 they became members of EIS, GSII, GHQ India, a rather interesting arrangement and one that worked very effectively.

Economic intelligence has been variously defined; a simple definition is "knowledge of the economy of a political entity." The collection of economic intelligence during World War II was similar to the collection of other forms of intelligence. Economic intelligence, ideally, consisted of "hard" data, for example, the amount and specific location of the production of economic goods and services. This contrasted with the "soft" nature of political and psychological intelligence. Much economic intelligence collected during World War II was in bits and pieces. These needed to be analyzed and fitted into a meaningful mosaic. Much of the collection of economic intelligence was a searching for economic facts, sometimes obscure and dull facts. There was very little derring-do in economic intelligence. I have been unable to find novels, histories or "I was there" books on economic intelligence during World War II. The intelligence officers of the Ministry of Economic Warfare and the Board of Economic Warfare took pride in their work and the contributions they were able to make in the pursuit of the war and in the planning of the peace.

The many forms of economic intelligence and their collection may be illustrated by my own personal activities with the Board of Economic Warfare and its successor agency, the Foreign Economic Administration, during World War II.

Economic intelligence is often found in published materials. In February 1942, shortly after I joined the Board of Economic Warfare we were able to obtain a library of Japanese yearbooks, economic surveys and journals which had been assembled by a Japanese research organization in New York. I had worked in this library some months before so that I knew of its existence and was familiar with its contents. The library gave us a very useful base of published materials on Japan.

The Board of Economic Warfare throughout the war supplemented this library with the acquisition of newly published materials. For example, the head of a Chinese economic agency in Chungking gave a farewell party for me as I was leaving China to return to Washington in February 1945. As a farewell gift, he gave me a copy of the Oriental Economist which had been published in Tokyo three weeks before and which had reached Chungking via Shanghai. I hand-carried this to Washington within the next week. The collection of published materials was rarely so rapid, but it was this basic economic data in published materials that enabled us to make estimates of many sectors of the Japanese economy.

Very similar to the current published materials were the wire service reports and the news broadcasts which emanated from Japan and Japanese-occupied areas. These were recorded, translated and disseminated by the information services of the United States and Britain. I read the Japanese Domei Press summaries almost every day during World War II. These included much general information and some economic intelligence. One had to read between the lines and to be cautious in giving credence to the propaganda which was included in this material. There were many significant materials which were not censored nor disguised. Misinformation was included but could readily be identified.

When I got to Chungking, China, in the summer of 1944 and was reorganizing our operations there, the local head of the American Office of War Information (OWI) kindly furnished me with a copy of the daily Domei radio news in English. The OWI taped this during the day time. He told me, incidentally, that the same channel was used for commercial Japanese language cable traffic to and from Tokyo and Shanghai at night. I asked to see some of this material which OWI had not bothered to record previously. I got some of it translated and it looked interesting. However, there was a real shortage of Japanese-English translators. I found some Chinese who knew English and others who knew Japanese. The same was also true of some Koreans. Therefore, I hired these people and set up two "lines" and we had the Japanese commercial intercepts translated into Chinese and then into English or into Korean and then into English.

We set up a filing system so that we could follow the messages from a single sender. I recall reading the intercepts one morning and finding an intercept that rang a bell. I looked up the file and read where some weeks before a Japanese business man in Shanghai had asked permission to return to the head office in Tokyo. Then he cabled that he had gotten passage on a ship. In a later message he named the ship. Then he cabled that he was leaving on such and such a date. Actually each of the messages was innocuous and passed the censor. However, when put together in sequence they revealed the exact name and date of a ship leaving Shanghai. I took the messages to the Navy Intelligence office near my office and spread them out. They took it from there and later told me a submarine had sunk the ship.

In another case we had hundreds of messages about the difficulties a Japanese company was having in developing a plant to process aluminum shales in north China. My friends in the Air Force in Chungking kept wanting to have me recommend the bombing of the facilities. I insisted that the new construction was wasting Japanese resources and that I would let them know when it was operating.

Actually, the war was over before the plant was finished. Its equipment was probably shipped off to the Soviet Union as "war reparations." These are good illustrations of the little bits and pieces that make up economic intelligence.

Though old fashioned techniques were used in the collection of economic intelligence, some newer techniques were also used, notably aerial photography. Though priority was given to photographs of military installations and topographic features, along with bomb damage assessments, we were able to get some air photo coverage of economic activities. Much, of course, depended upon the correct interpretations of the air photos. I recall that in New Delhi my British opposite number in the Economic Intelligence Section brought in the managers of the tin mines in Burma. We had gotten pictures of these mines. (By the way, the British had close working relationships with British companies and bringing in the managers to see and comment on these classified pictures was not considered strange.) One of the managers pleaded with us to let him parachute in to his mine. Another got me off in the corner and urged me to say that his plant was operating and thus should be a target for destruction. I had to tell him that Japan had captured so much stockpiled tin in Burma at the start of the war that by this time in 1943, it was a waste of energy for the Japanese to be operating his plant. He had hoped that his facilities would be destroyed so that he could have a new facility after the war!

Though personal observers or spies (now known in the jargon as HUMINT) are often considered glamorous and given headlines, they were not a major source of economic intelligence. I hired a Chinese agent, a former jockey, who went down the Yangtze River from Chungking for me every month or so and collected data on the Tayeh iron mines near Hankow. These were being exploited by the Japanese and were something of an indication of Japan's industrial climate. The first time he came back, he told me, as I recall, that there were two 30-car trains coming out of the mines every day. I told him that this was little help unless we knew the size of the cars. The next time he came back he measured out hand spans on the floor and wall of my office and we converted the measurements to the size of cars and the tons of iron ore they carried. He was doing some smuggling on the side and was a useful and not very expensive agent.

We interviewed many people and gathered their knowledge of economic matters. I had a luncheon every week in Chungking for agricultural and other economists and another bi-weekly luncheon for geographers. They appreciated the good food and we gained useful information. When I was in New Delhi I sent out a request for economic information to American missionaries and business-men who had been in

Burma and were then in India. I got a number of replies, including one by a former professor at the University of Rangoon who said he knew nothing of the economy of Burma, but if I wanted to know about the earth worms of Burma, he was the world authority!

Personal sources of economic intelligence, or HUMINT, included prisoners of war. There were not many Japanese surrendering on the Burma front, but a few did and the British imprisoned them in the Red Fort in Delhi. We were able to interrogate some of them. One of my colleagues had great success with one Japanese who drew a detailed map of a factory in Nagoya, previously unknown to us, where he had worked before being drafted into the Japanese army. He provided an interesting case study of the problems in the industrial economy of Japan. At the end of two or three weeks of interrogation we put on a sort of show to which we invited British and American officers, so that they could understand the value of economic intelligence from POW sources. At the end of the session one of the British officers noted that the map drawn by the Japanese POW was lacking any indication of anti-aircraft gun emplacements. The Japanese POW drew himself up to his full 5 foot 2 and said: "Sir, that is a military secret."

Finally, there were some special sources of economic intelligence which were the result of electronic surveillance and code breaking. These were usually called by special names: ULTRA by the British and MAGIC by the Americans. They are now grouped together as SIGINT, Signals Intelligence, in contrast to HUMINT, or human intelligence. These were highly classified during World War II. Only recently has their existence even been acknowledged. Now there is quite a bit of open literature on SIGINT.[5]

Most of the special material was tactical intelligence which was of crucial importance in the European theater of war. In 1944 when I was in New Delhi and was getting ready to go to Southeast Asia Command in Ceylon, I was "signed on" to the use of ULTRA by a British officer. Actually I was possibly the only person working for the Board of Economic Warfare who had access to this material. My superiors in Washington did not know that I had "signed on" to this intelligence and I could not tell them of it.

There was not a great deal of economic intelligence in this special material. Few military people were interested in economic intelligence and the priority was given to tactical and strategic intelligence and to diplomatic channels, "the reading of other gentlemen's mail." There was a very strong feeling that no one should use this special material as a sole source, for fear that to do so might result in a change in the codes of the enemy. When this material was used in the shooting down of Admiral Yamamoto, the brilliant Japanese naval strategist, on April 18, 1943, there was great concern in the intelligence community that this source had been compromised.[6]

While I was at Southeast Asia Command I came across some excellent special material in ULTRA on Japanese oil production in Southeast Asia. This was sort of buried, as I recall, in monthly reports that went back to Tokyo in code as a low priority in Japanese military channels. I wanted to use these figures but I could not do so since it was a single source. Therefore, I collected all the available economic intelligence from all sources on Japanese oil production in Southeast Asia. These included snippets from the Domei Press, pre-war production figures, reports from oil companies, some ground and air photo intelligence and some translated articles from Japanese magazines and yearbooks. I put all of this data on a map of oil fields in Southeast Asia. Then in red pencil I put the yearly output figures converted from the monthly figures in the special source. Then I attempted to reconcile the production figures from the diversified sources to those given in the ULTRA materials. Finally, I redid the maps and wrote a report ostensibly based on the non-special materials, suitably adjusted or juggled.

The Director of Intelligence for the Southeast Asia Command, a British marine general, liked my report very much. He arranged for me to give an oral briefing to Lord Louis Montbatten and his staff. At the end of my 20-minute presentation an American, Lieutenant-General Wheeler, head of Services of Supply, said that he had recently been in Washington where he had talked to some oil company executives. They had given him some guesstimates which differed considerably from some of my figures. He went after me for a lack of consistency: in one instance I had estimated the oil production at 35% of pre-war production and yet at another field I used a figure of 65%. Of course, I had done so in order to bring the figures close to the production figures revealed in the special source, but I could not tell him that. The Director of Intelligence came to my rescue and suggested that I talk to General Wheeler privately; he added, looking directly at Lord Louis, that I had worked hard in looking for special sources of material. Lord Louis caught the implication, only half of the persons in the room probably had access to ULTRA, and closed off the discussion. After the meeting broke up the Director whispered in Lord Louis' ear and Lord Louis, in turn, went across to General Wheeler and told him something.

The next day I went to see General Wheeler and he was very affable and gave me the figures he had gotten. I told him nothing of my real source but I reconciled or juggled my figures with more care and to his satisfaction. I sent my report up to New Delhi and hence back to Washington. My superiors in Washington thought it was just a clever amalgam of intelligence materials. They did not know it was really based on excellent Japanese sources to which they did not have access.

When I went to Chungking in the summer of 1944, I "signed off" and never used this special material again. The Japanese never did believe that we had broken their codes. My "signing off" was, of course, in keeping with one of the principles of intelligence of any type: "the doctrine of the need to know." Intelligence officers and agencies were remarkably ignorant about some things because of this doctrine.

As illustrated by my own personal experience, the collection of economic intelligence was based on many diverse sources. Some of the sources were very open, others were highly classified. It was the pattern that emerged from the bits and pieces that became meaningful. It was sometimes argued that economic intelligence should only be collected by persons who had a broad knowledge of the economy of the enemy, but such persons were very rare. Most of us who were involved in economic intelligence were learning on the job. Few of us had language skills. We came from many different backgrounds, ranging from news reporters to archaeologists. Perfectionists were rare in our company, since we were daily called upon to make judgments on limited data. Few of us had training in theoretical economics. I was an economic geographer with an interest in the Far East; this background was very helpful in my work on Japan and Japanese-occupied areas.

Economic intelligence did not stand alone. It was a part of the total intelligence effort of the United States and Britain during World War II.[7] There was a considerable amount of give and take among the intelligence agencies. For example, we developed a Joint Intelligence Collection Agency (JICA) in Chungking, so that the intelligence could be distributed within Chungking and sent back in a single copy to Washington where it could be copied and sent to various agencies. It was a very efficient system.

The best economic intelligence was "hard" intelligence with accurate economic data. It was rare that this desired accuracy could be obtained, so that some economic intelligence was "soft," similar to political, social and psychological intelligence. The estimates made of Japanese economic activities on the basis of the economic intelligence which was gathered, however, were remarkably accurate.

CHAPTER II

THE PACIFIC WAR

The Pacific War, as it was called by the Japanese, was started by the Japanese attack on Pearl Harbor on December 7, 1941, "the day of infamy." To many people, the devastation caused by the Japanese attack was the result of a failure in intelligence. Many books have been written on this subject.[8]

When the Japanese attacked Pearl Harbor in 1941, the United States was sadly lacking in economic intelligence on Japan. Soon, efforts were made to gather such intelligence and analyze it to make judgments about Japan's economic strengths and weaknesses. There were many sources of economic intelligence and these have been discussed in the previous chapter.

Throughout World War II, I was in the economic intelligence business, concentrating on Japan and Japanese-occupied areas. I served in Washington, New Delhi, India, Kandy, Ceylon and Chungking, China with the Board of Economic Warfare and its successor agency, the Foreign Economic Administration. The primary aim of the economic intelligence sections with which I worked was to provide knowledge of the economies of our enemies: Germany, Italy and Japan, so that our agencies could use economic warfare means effectively. It made no sense, for example, to set up preclusive purchasing of commodities in satellite, neutral or occupied countries, like tungsten in Spain, gall nuts in Turkey or cotton in China, if the enemy had plentiful supplies or substitute sources. The collection, analysis, dissemination and exploitation of economic intelligence during World War II was of value to other agencies, notably the armed forces.

The Japanese after their victory at Pearl Harbor quickly advanced into Southeast Asia, conquering vast territories with dense populations. The Japanese Army and Navy often competed over their programs in these areas. They sought to over-come these rivalries and to establish their hegemony over these areas by a vision of a Greater East Asia Co-Prosperity Sphere. Economic intelligence in Southeast Asia was very spotty. On some activities undertaken by the Japanese, for example, the building of the railroad from Thailand to Burma, there was little "hard" information available, until it was almost completed. In other cases, like shipping activities in Hong Kong, we had excellent information such as scale profiles of every ship that went in or out of the harbor.

The Allied strategy was to stop any further advances by the Japanese into India, toward Australia and into Central and South China. The Battle of Midway of June 1942, incidentally an American intelligence triumph through the use of MAGIC as contrasted with the intelligence failure of Pearl Harbor, stopped the Japanese in the central Pacific Ocean areas.[9] The landings at Gaudalcanal in August 1942 halted Japan's advance toward Australia. Large numbers of British and Indian forces defended the Burma frontier, though weather, terrain and malarial mosquitoes were almost equally important in stopping the Japanese advances. The Japanese held the rail lines and the cities of central and southern China but, though there were vast numbers of troops involved in China, there was not much large-scale fighting.

One of the strategies that the United States considered after the devastation at Pearl Harbor and the Japanese invasions of Southeast Asia was based on the concept that Japan's economy was made of two zones: an Inner Zone of the Japanese Islands, Korea, Manchuria and North China and an Outer Zone of Formosa, South China, and the lands, islands and peninsulas of Southeast Asia.

The gross strategy of the United States was to cut off the Outer Zone from the Inner Zone. In the Outer Zone were strategic materials such as oil, iron ore, bauxite and various metals, zinc, lead and tin--plus large quantities of rice and vegetable oils. With these resources, it was possible that in time Japan could build its economic and military power. The Japanese hoped that this would make them so formidable that they could negotiate a peace with the United States. They did not understand the psychological effect of Pearl Harbor on the American people nor the war production capacity of the United States.

One obvious way to break the connection between the Inner Zone and the Outer Zone was to go after Japanese merchant shipping. At the start of the war the Japanese had 6.6 million tons of ships over 100 tons. They captured another 0.8 million tons and then built 3.1 million tons, mainly in 1943 and 1944. This gave them a total of 10.5 million tons. The Board of Economic Warfare (BEW) when I joined it in early February of 1942 was gathering data on Japanese merchant shipping and with that data and other materials made a projection of Japan's need for merchant tonnage. We estimated that to tie the economy of the Outer Zone to that of the Inner Zone the Japanese would need 4 to 5 million tons of merchant shipping. Thus, the Japanese had a comfortable capacity from their pre-war and captured tonnage. The BEW projection was based on three assumptions: the efficient use of its merchant marine by the Japanese, the setting-up and use of ship repair facilities in Southeast Asia, and no rivalry between the Japanese Army and the Japanese Navy. In fact, we began to realize as we gathered more economic intelligence that none of these three assumptions was valid. Japan was inefficiently wasting much of its merchant marine. The American strategy of going after Japanese ships began to pay off. The United States built submarines and attack boats; we developed explosive mines which could be sown from the air and which were nasty in their variable timing devices. To skip ahead, on 15 July 1945 the Japanese merchant tonnage had "sunk" to 2.2 million tons, some of which was isolated in Southeast Asia and some of which was in repair yards in Japan.

As American military strength increased a number of strategic decisions needed to be made. One was that instead of rolling back the Japanese, enemy garrisons and strong points, such as Rabaul and Truk, would be by-passed. Thus, by the spring of 1945 there were many Japanese out-posts in Southeast Asia which had large numbers of troops, but these troops could not be effective offensively. Some of these outposts had severe shortages of food and equipment, with troops suffering from malnutrition and malaria. Nevertheless, the Japanese continued to fight fanatically if attacked.

A significant difference between the United States Army and Navy strategy was on the manner in which the Outer Zone should be severed from the Inner Zone. Some Navy strategists wanted to by-pass the Philippines and take Formosa and from there make landings in southern Kyushu, a two-jump strategy. General MacArthur, the Army commander in the Southwest Pacific wanted to return to the Philippines, from there land in Okinawa and then invade southern Kyushu, a three-jump strategy, and this strategy was the one that was followed.

On April 1, 1945, Easter Sunday, American troops made a massive landing on Okinawa. This was the final action which cut off the Outer Zone from the Inner Zone.[10] Okinawa was no soft target, for the Japanese had developed a dogged defense based on the limestone caves, ravines and tunnels in southern Okinawa. It took the American forces 92 days to advance 22 miles. Finally, the Japanese commanders committed suicide in a cave with American troops pinned down only a few yards away.

In the spring of 1945 a new element was becoming dominant in the Pacific War: the use of long range aircraft, the B-29's. This airplane was designed for pin-point bombing of distant targets. I recall an Air Corps colonel saying to me in 1944 in Chungking: "You tell me where the blank factory is and I'll drop a blank bomb down its blank chimney." Air fields were constructed by massive human labor in Chengtu in western China. After Saipan and Tinian in the Marianas were captured on July 9, 1944, air fields were constructed there which were closer to Japan than Chengtu. The capture of Iwo-Jima, halfway between Saipan and Tokyo, on March 26, 1945, was very bloody but very necessary for it provided a haven for

American planes returning from air raids on Japan. The B-29 attacks from Chengtu and, later, from Saipan enabled the United States to strike economic and industrial targets in Japan, China, and Manchuria late in 1944 and early in 1945. These air raids were quite successful, but still did not succeed in destroying Japan's economy.

In early March 1945, a major change in tactics took place. Rather than precision attacks on industrial and military targets, the B-29's from Saipan were used for massive incendiary attacks on Japanese urban areas. These attacks destroyed many of the home workshops which were vital in Japan's economic geography. The incendiary bombs were nefarious devices. Some of them had spikes which drove down into the tatami floors and then shot incendiary gel up under the roofs of the tinder-box houses. Most notable was the fire raid on Tokyo on the night of March 9-10 in which a circle of fire was developed which built on itself. There were an estimated 100,000 casualties and a large section of northeastern Tokyo and other sections as well were destroyed in that one air raid.

In the spring and summer of 1945, the Japanese economy was thus deteriorating. The Outer Zone had been separated from the Inner Zone and the Inner Zone was being laid waste by incendiary air raids and the aerial mining of harbors. The homeland of Japan was subject to devastating aerial attacks. Many of their Navy ships were sunk. Though there were large numbers of troops, more than two million, in Manchuria, China and Southeast Asia, these Japanese troops were ill-supplied and were largely in defensive positions. The economy of Japan was crumbling and severe shortages were developing. The American strategy had been successful and the Japanese were facing defeat.

CHAPTER III

JAPAN'S ECONOMY IN 1945

The events of the Pacific War were summarized in the Weekly Summary of the Joint Intelligence Committee in the spring and summer of 1945. The Weekly Summary also contained a number of articles which gave background information on specific economic activities carried on by the Japanese or upon areas which were of significance to Japan. These articles were written by me and my colleagues in the Enemy Branch of the Foreign Economic Administration. I was the FEA representative on the Joint Intelligence Staff during this period.

The Joint Intelligence Committee was made up of the heads of the various intelligence agencies. It met only occasionally. The Joint Intelligence Staff, in contrast, met on a daily basis and acted as a unified agency for the writing of the Weekly Summary and of other papers requested by the Joint Chiefs of Staff. The Joint Intelligence Staff, as I recall, was made up of two captains from Navy Intelligence, two colonels from G-2, Army Intelligence, two colonels from A-2, Air Intelligence, and single representatives from the Department of State, the Office of Strategic Services and the Foreign Economic Administration. In addition there was an Executive Secretary, an Editor, some administrative personnel and an excellent secretarial staff. It was a remarkably cohesive group and we all had high respect for each other.

The purpose of the Weekly Summary was to highlight "the military, political, economic and psychological situation." The first part of a forty page issue was arranged geographically by theaters of war giving information on the status of military actions. The second part was concerned with the individual events or trends which were of significance. The third part, what we called "the back of the book," was devoted to Special Articles which gave background information. These were printed in smaller type and each of the three or four Special Articles were usually two or three pages in length. The events of the week were given focus and emphasis in the first two sections. The Special Articles enabled the Joint Intelligence Staff to give attention in more depth and to highlight strategic areas, such as Korea, Hokkaido or Kyushu. The Special Articles on the economy of these areas were some times paralleled by articles on the military geography of the areas. The Special Articles added a useful and interesting supplement to the Weekly Summary.

The Weekly Summary was classified as SECRET. Though I thought from time to time that a couple of my colleagues had access to SIGINT, Signals Intelligence, we never mentioned the existence of this. Occasionally one of my colleagues would insist that he thought his material was correct, he never gave the source and we did not press him for it. By not overtly using SIGINT, or MAGIC, and using only SECRET and lower classified materials, we enjoyed a lot more freedom. It was possible to distribute the Weekly Summary widely among those who were making policy.

The Joint Intelligence Staff had a regular schedule in preparing the Weekly Summary. On Tuesday mornings we had a preliminary run-through of the materials provided from the different intelligence agencies. We sometimes requested further materials or Special Articles. On Wednesday we went over word-by-word the first draft of the material. On Thursday mornings we could make last minute additions and up-dates. The Editor then gave it a final reading for style and format. He hand-carried it to the Government Printing Office on late Thursday afternoon. On Friday mornings in printed form it was on the desk of the President and on the desks of other high military and civilian officials. It was the elite intelligence summary in the United States.

The notes and articles in the Weekly Summary were without any attribution to agencies or individuals. The Joint Intelligence Staff which prepared it was not mentioned; it was a publication of the Joint Intelligence Committee, though the members of that Committee did not see it until it was in print. Only rarely were references made to sources. The Joint Intelligence Staff took pride in the readability of the Weekly Summary; each of us made corrections for content and style. I recall early in my tenure on the Staff that I suggested a change in a report submitted by the Navy; this was somewhat of a no-no, for the Navy was the senior service. The sentence noted: "The present low state to which the Japanese navy has fallen." I suggested the substitution of the word "sunk" for "fallen" and gained the acceptance of my peers from then on.

The background articles were usually submitted on Monday or Tuesday morning. There was some discussion of the merits of the proposed Special Articles. In some cases they were rejected because of length or content. Those that were accepted were revised, especially for accuracy and readability. In particular there was an effort to edit out technical language and to highlight the significance of the material.

The Weekly Summary is now declassified and copies may be xeroxed at the Military Archives Division of the National Archives in Washington. Twelve of the Special Articles are reproduced in an Appendix at the back of this book in the chronological order in which they appeared in the Weekly Summary. Brief introductions to them may be useful.

The first article deals with the Bawdwin Mines in northern Burma. This was an important source of lead and zinc for the Japanese. There was a constant effort to collect firm economic intelligence on what had happened to the stockpiles and the level of production. This "final analysis" was based in part on a report by an FEA non-ferrous metals expert who had visited the Bawdwin Mines shortly after the Japanese withdrew. The exact economic intelligence on the Bawdwin Mines was always in dispute between the British and Americans. This article was aimed at settling the questions about what had happened to this source of strategic metals.

A short article in the next issue, #122, 10 May 1945, on "The Development of Aluminous Shales in Northern China," is, in contrast to the article on the Bawdwin Mines, much more speculative. I had been in Chungking, China and had been following the developments of these sources of aluminum. The article referred to ground reports and aerial photographs which I had arranged to have taken. The article notes that "no installation for the electrolytic production of metallic aluminum has been erected."

The next article in #122, 10 May 1945, on "The Location of Japan's Industrial War-making Capacity," is a rather routine compilation of the major components of Japanese war industries. It is noted that "80 to 90 percent of Japan's industrial war-making potential is located in the main Japanese islands." This article was followed up in the next week, #123, 17 May 1945, by an article on the possibilities of transferring some of the industrial war-making potential to the Asiatic mainland. There had been a lot of Japanese radio broadcasts about this possibility and the article attempts to sort out the situation. The Japanese had been shipping to the mainland some "idle mining and basic industrial and chemical equipment in order to increase the production of essential raw materials. . . " The expansion of "the production of munitions, as well as aircraft and parts, on the Asiatic mainland" was possible but would be "limited by the availability of surplus machinery and tools on the mainland and in Japan." It is noted that the present capacity on the mainland "for the production of aircraft, shipping and some other essential war needs is relatively of negligible consequence."

The two articles on Japanese war production capacity within the home islands and on the adjacent Asiatic mainland were followed by another general article on a key factor in Japan's war economy: "The Importance and Vulnerability of Japanese Lines of Communication," Issue #124, 24 May 1945. The Japanese railroad system is briefly described. The article stresses that "the Japanese railroad system is much more susceptible to air attack than were any of the European systems, owing to its comparatively small size, its predominantly single tract routes, the scarcity of alternative routes and rail centers, and the abundance of major engineering structures." The article notes that "Japan's road system is relatively unimportant except for local movements." Having said that "the very great importance to Japan of ocean shipping is well known," the article stresses that the shipping routes of the Yellow Sea, the Straits of Tsushima and the Sea of Japan "will be of the greatest importance to Japan." It is pointed out that "The tremendous concentrations of shipping in the Shimonoseki-Wakamatsu and Osaka-Kobe areas of the Inland Sea should prove particularly vulnerable to air attacks. Mining operations and attacks on port facilities and ferry terminals will add greatly to Japan's shipping difficulties." Having stressed the importance of the ports in the Straits of Tsushima, it was logical to have an article a couple of weeks later devoted solely to "the Importance of the port of Fusan," Issue #127, 14 June 1945. This brief article on the port in southeastern Korea describes its facilities and calls it a "vital center for trade and shipping between the mainland and Japan."

In the months of July, August and early September, a series of articles on the economies of different areas was published in the Weekly Summary. These background articles followed a somewhat similar format in analyzing the importance of these areas to the economy of Japan. The areas on which articles are published are listed below:

Inner Mongolia	#130	5 July 1945
Korea	#132	19 July 1945
Kyushu	#133	26 July 1945
Karafuto	#137	23 August 1945
Hokkaido	#139	6 September 1945
Manchuria	#140	13 September 1945

Each of these areas had strategic importance as Japan was faced by the invasion of the United States and of the USSR. Kyushu and Hokkaido were part of the Japanese home islands but they were separate islands. Korea and Karafuto were colonies. Inner Mongolia and Manchuria were under puppet regimes of Japan. The contributions which they made to the Japanese war economy varied considerably. The articles on Korea and on Hokkaido were longer and contained a great deal of data. The article on Manchuria was published some weeks after the invasion by the USSR on August 9. The article concludes with this paragraph:

> The economic future of Manchuria will depend to a large extent upon Chinese and Soviet policy. The resources of the land and people and the advanced

industrial development will be of great aid to the postwar industrial growth of China. The agricultural resources will be of benefit to the U.S.S.R. The uprooting of Japanese economic control will be a necessary preliminary to the reorientation of Manchuria toward the economy of China."

CHAPTER IV

JAPAN'S ECONOMIC COLLAPSE IN 1945

The Weekly Summary of the Joint Intelligence Committee summarized the events of the previous week as they influenced "the military, political, economic and psychological situation." Notes and Special Articles discussed the economic collapse of Japan in the spring and summer of 1945. The capture of Okinawa, the sinking of Japanese merchant tonnage and the B-29 air raids on Japanese cities were significant events which were noted in the Weekly Summary. Much of the economic intelligence material came from the Enemy Branch of the Foreign Economic Administration. As already noted, I was the FEA representative on the Joint Intelligence Staff during this period. Some of the economic materials came from the Department of State and the Office of Strategic Services; I had the responsibility of editing this material. The Joint Intelligence Staff worked as a group and there was no attribution to individuals or agencies in the Weekly Summary which the Staff prepared.

An interesting summary of the Japanese economy was given in the Weekly Summary, #123, 17 May 1945. It noted that "During the last six months the Japanese economy has deteriorated more rapidly than at any time since the beginning of the war in the Pacific." This article is more broadly based than most of the articles which were included in "the back of the book" of the Weekly Summary. It is reproduced in full at the end of this chapter.

Some quotes from the article will give an indication of the status of the Japanese economy at this time.

> The weather was said to have been the coldest in 25 years, severe earthquakes occurred in Hokkaido and in central Japan, and Allied air raids steadily mounted in scale. The dispersal of war plants, evacuation, and the destruction of housing facilities in air raids has caused severe dislocation not only in the cities but also in the rural areas receiving the flow of refugees. . . . The people, caught between inflated costs, high taxes, and compulsory savings, were finding it hard to make ends meet in spite of increased salaries. . .

> On March 10 males between 12 and 40 were made eligible to call for home defense as well as for war production. . . . Evacuation has reduced Tokyo's 1944 population of over 7 million to less than 4 million. . . . The populace is constantly told (by radio) that the war may last 12 or 20 years and that 100,000,000 Japanese must be killed before Japan can be defeated."

One of the most important elements in the Japanese war economy was merchant shipping. It was by this means that the Japanese expected to obtain the raw materials from the "Outer Zone" of Southeast Asia which had been captured at the start of the war. Merchant shipping was also significant in tieing together the economy of the "Inner Zone" of Central and North China, Manchuria, Korea and the homeland of Japan. The Weekly Summary, #128, 21 June 1945, had a note on "Recent Developments in Japanese Shipping Control." On 1 May 1945 an Inspectorate General of Marine Transportation was created so that there would be "Joint Army and Navy control established over both operation and administration of all shipping and port facilities." A Special Article in the Weekly Summary, #133, 26 July 1945, dealt with the "Further Deterioration of the Japanese Merchant Shipping Situation." This was accompanied by five appendices giving tables of estimated tonnages in different categories. (These appendices have not been reproduced.)

The Special Article notes that "In the fall of 1944 the Japanese had sufficient merchant shipping to supply their home islands with necessary commodities for maintaining their war industries or for supporting further military operations overseas, but not for doing both. The Army-dominated Government decided on the latter course. . ." Because many of the military convoys were sunk, the Japanese merchant tonnage was reduced substantially. Thus on 15 July 1945 it was estimated that "the total tonnage afloat of Japanese ships over 100 gross tons was about 2,200,000 gross tons." Moreover, the article points out that many of these ships were undergoing or awaiting repairs and "over 10 percent of the remaining tonnage is still in the Netherlands East Indies and Southeast Asia." The Special Article concludes with this sentence: "The Japanese food situation has also been affected by the shortage of ships, and while stockpiles and increased home production may alleviate conditions somewhat, it is clear that there is no permanent solution to the Japanese dilemma."

The food situation of Japan was indeed in dire straits. In a note in the Weekly Summary, #123, 17 May 1945, the measures of the Japanese "for the protection of crops from Allied air raids and for the increase of farm production" are noted. Some of the rice for Japan was imported from Korea and Korea, in turn, imported low grade cereals from Manchuria. The Weekly Summary, #129, 28 June 1945, noted that "poor crops, increased Korean consumption and transport difficulties" had progressively curtailed the Korean contributions of food to Japan. A Special Article on "The Food Shortage in Japan," Weekly Summary, #136, 16 August 1945 stated that "The gradual deterioration of the Japanese food situation which began in 1939-40 has continued at an accelerated rate. Japan is now facing a very serious food shortage in the home islands." The situation "will become much more critical in the month of September before the new rice harvest can be reaped." Evidently there was some relief, for in a short note in the Weekly Summary, #139, 30 August 1945, after the Japanese had surrendered, there is mention of two factors that would "tend to ease the food problem." One of these was the ability of Japan's fishing fleet to resume operations and the other was that "the demobilization of the Army and war workers will eliminate the extra rations formerly granted these groups..."

In the spring and summer of 1945 a number of financial moves were taken to try to avert the economic collapse of Japan. These were not very successful. A note in the Weekly Summary, #123, 17 May 1945, discussed "the Emergency Munitions Financing Law, which assigns particular banks to meet the needs of specific munitions companies." Two weeks later, the Weekly Summary, #125, 31 May 1945, notes that a "Law Pertaining to Acutely Vital Affairs of Wartime-essential Personnel served to keep the Japanese, both employers and laborers, on their jobs in essential war industries and on distributing them as the authorities wish." The issue of the Weekly Summary, #133, 26 July 1945 had a note on "Inflation in Japan." This was based in part on Japanese broadcasts by the Japanese Finance Minister who warned that if inflationary pressures remain unchanged, "it will greatly affect the foundation of the Japanese fighting strength." In a rare instance of self-criticism, he said that "the present inflationary tendency is primarily attributable to enormous Government expenditures."

One of the very interesting developments in the economy of Japan in the summer of 1945 was the formation of eight economic administrative regions in Japan. The three islands of Hokkaido, Shikoku and Kyushu were each made economic regions and the island of Honshu was divided into five regions, each centered on a major city; the cities were Sendai, Tokyo, Nagoya, Osaka and Hiroshima. This regional scheme was first promulgated in a Wartime Emergency Measures Bill of 12 June 1945. The Bill was discussed in a note in the Weekly Summary, #127, 14 June 1945. The Bill provided that "In the event of a breakdown of communications through invasion or enemy action, each of the eight regions of Japan proper could become autonomous." This was a rather frightening prospect in my view, so that I kept writing notes about it. One lengthy note in a Weekly Summary a week later, #128, 21 June 1945, discussed the functioning of these regions and the powers of the Superintendents-General appointed to head these regions. The Japanese Army and Navy commands were re-organized in order to conform to these regions. As noted in the Weekly Summary, #129, 28 June 1945, "the banks and large Japanese concerns--Mitsui, Mitsubishi, Sumitomo and others--are taking similar steps for regional administration. The present regional decentralization is occasioned not only by the fear that the transportation and communication links within Japan may be destroyed, but that Tokyo, the nerve center, may be made completely ineffective."

Associated with this regional rearrangement of Japan's economy was the necessity for evacuation of the major cities of Japan. An article in the Weekly Summary, #125, 31 May 1945 discusses the evacuation measures undertaken in Japan. Much of this evacuation seems to have been voluntary, but the Japanese government had "emergency measures" which they could use. The persons who left the cities were assigned rural areas to which they were to go. "Upon their arrival in these rural areas the evacuees are quartered in temples, national schools, and barracks. . ." They were to be trained "in the raising of potatoes, grains, vegetables, chickens, and rabbits." All was not smooth in the evacuation system and a Japanese government report declared that "the population of large cities are showing extreme tendencies toward scattering."

The Premier of Japan, Admiral Suzuki, had said in early June, according to a note in the Weekly Summary, that the Japanese had "all the advantages of geography and the solidarity of the people" in resisting invasion. He went on to say "Judging from the trends within enemy countries and considering the developments in the international situation, I cannot help feel strongly that the only way for us to do is to fight to the last." This was a constant theme in the Japanese propaganda statements during the summer of 1945.

In the Weekly Summary of 31 May 1945 a Special Article dealt with Signs of Deterioration in Japanese Military Morale and started with this sentence: "The will of the Japanese soldiers to resist and their disinclination to surrender, even under the most adverse circumstances, continue to be strong." The Special Article concluded with this sentence: "Nevertheless, there is abundant evidence that the conviction is beginning to spread among Japanese troops everywhere, not merely that particular territories are irrevocably lost, but also that the whole war is lost."

There was in the summer of 1945 a deep concern in the Joint Intelligence Staff and elsewhere in the United States government over the size of the Japanese forces. Taking the figures from the battles of Okinawa and Iwo-Jima, it was estimated that the American landings in southern Kyushu and later on the Kanto Plain near Tokyo would cost over a million American lives and to conquer all of Japan would take three years of fighting with great loss of American lives. This was sobering.

Some fresh studies were made and disseminated in the Weekly Summary of the manpower available to Japan. As of 1 June 1945 it was estimated that there were in the Japanese home islands, 3.7 million men in the Japanese Army, 350,000 in the Air Force and 750,000 in the Navy. There were, in addition, 10.6 million men between 17 and 44 years of age. This manpower had been used in essential industry and agriculture. Aerial bombing and blockade had resulted in the release of many industrial workers. Some of these were needed for civil defense activities such as fighting fires, clearing bombed areas and so on. There still remained a surplus of a million workers. In addition, the natural growth of population, continued mobilization of women and school children for work on farms and the return of men invalided out of the armed forces furnished another million men. The transfer of two million men into the Japanese armed forces was therefore feasible. Thus the Japanese had a formidable mass of persons who could be organized to resist invasion and be called up as reservists in the pattern used in Okinawa. The defeat of such a large Japanese army was daunting to the United States.

Japan: Winter of 1944-1945

During the last 6 months the Japanese economy has deteriorated more rapidly than at any time since the beginning of war in the Pacific. For the average Japanese the winter just past was one of constant strain. The weather was said to have been the coldest in 25 years, severe earthquakes occurred in Hokkaido and in central Japan, and Allied air raids steadily mounted in scale. The dispersal of war plants, evacuation, and the destruction of housing facilities in air raids has caused severe dislocation not only in the cities but also in the rural areas receiving the flow of refugees.

Every phase of Japanese life has been constricted by the war, and the Government has demanded increased sacrifices of all kinds from the citizenry, including a 7-day work week. The first tendency toward dangerous currency inflation since the start of the war followed a recent steep rise in war expenditure. The people, caught between inflated costs, high taxes, and compulsory savings, are finding it hard to make ends meet in spite of increased salaries.

Despite claims that Japan's existing labor supply is sufficient, the Government has continued to take measures to enlarge it. On 10 March males between 12 and 40 were made subject to call for home defense as well as for war production. Previously these groups only could be called up for work in certain essential industries. Much emphasis has been placed on monthly production quotas in war plants, and in November, Tokyo promoted the "special-attack spirit" as a propaganda device designed to inspire civilians as well as the military to make greater sacrifices for the war. As a result, many factories have organized special units whose members pledge to extend their working hours and outdo the monthly quotas.

Unmarried women are widely employed in food and munitions production, shipyards, offices, aircraft plants, and the transportation industry. School and university schedules are closely geared to make the fullest use of the student group as a source of labor for farming, mining, and munitions factories. School children, for example, are said to be growing potatoes and rice as well as carrying on the work formerly done by janitors. They are told not to play with toys, but to study and work.

Evacuation has reduced Tokyo's 1944 population of over 7 million to less than 4 million. Compulsory mass evacuation measures, with special emphasis on children and nonessential adults, were intensified after the heavy March air raids demonstrated the complete inadequacy of shelters and defense precautions. Measures taken to restrain essential workers from fleeing the city indicate a high degree of confusion and terror. Many people have been forced to live in cellars or shacks constructed from debris. Family life has been severely disrupted.

The procurement of such essentials as food, fuel, and clothing has been a great problem for the people of Japan. Despite fairly successful attempts to achieve self-sufficiency within the inner zone, Japan still depends on imports for 20 percent of her food supply. Now that supplies from the southern regions have been cut off, Japan will become increasingly dependent on stocks accumulated over the last 2 or 3 years to maintain the present level of consumption. Japanese farmers are being heavily pressed to increase the production of their fields despite a critical lack of fertilizer needed to enrich the poor farming soil. But on the whole they are better off than city-dwellers. Besides having less to fear from air raids, the farmers alone in all Japan go to bed at night with full stomachs. In the cities the grounds of many schools and temples are being transformed into vegetable gardens. The lawns of at least one zoo are growing food, and its cages have been adapted for the raising of rabbits, goats, and hogs.

Fish is scarce because of insufficient equipment and labor, and meat and dairy products, always minor items in the Japanese diet, have disappeared almost completely. Scientists are continually experimenting with new foods. Dolphin meat has been found to be the best tasting of all the sea mammals, while the skin can be used for shoes and the brain oil for lubrication purposes. Seals and sharks have been found to be very nutritious. A Japanese commentator who said, "I cannot say that our food is ideal," may have been thinking of the new ersatz sugar, the synthetic beer, or the table butter made from silkworms.

Although there have been no serious epidemics, public health in Japan has declined as a result of malnutrition, inordinate working hours, and poor housing, heating, and clothing. Tuberculosis, for example, has been increasing, especially among factory workers. Large-scale evacuation of cities has aggravated the health situation.

People are crowded into small villages where unhygienic conditions prevail and no adequate heating facilities exist. Throughout Japan there is a serious scarcity of fuel, woolens, overcoats, and shoes, and a lack of doctors, dentists, and druggists.

The Government's conservation program has affected practically every aspect of city life. Restaurants have been closed down by the hundreds and have been replaced to some extent by community kitchens operated by women volunteers. Newspapers have been limited to two pages except on special days, when four are permitted, and large numbers of periodicals have been discontinued. Tokyo's rail service has been greatly curtailed, with tickets issued only to military and Government personnel on urgent business. Streetcars haul vegetables and fish in addition to passengers, and seats have been removed to accommodate more people. There are repeated drives for metals of all kinds, and children are urged to collect such items as fallen leaves for fertilizer and orange peels, which are said to be useful in the preparation of a certain drug. The textile shortage has increasingly forced women to substitute trousers for the *kimono* and the wide *obie*.

Such entertainment as is available in Japan appears to offer little real relaxation. Newspapers contain little but war news slanted to incite the Japanese citizen to work harder, and the available movies deal almost exclusively with war topics. With a reduced number of movies and night clubs as a result of air raids and Government edicts, the Japanese are turning more and more to the radio for entertainment, but even here they complain about the excessive "sermons and preaching." The populace is constantly told that the war may last 10 or 20 years and that "100,000,000 Japanese must be killed before Japan can be defeated." One of the most popular forms of relaxation for the average Japanese, the public bath, is restricted and overcrowded owing to manpower and fuel shortages. Although the number of national saloons has increased, Tokyo citizens have to stand in lines of 200 to 300 to buy an expensive drink of *sake* or other liquor.

Recent Developments in Japanese Shipping Control

Sea-borne commerce is essential to Japan's active prosecution of war, and an increasing trend toward state control of Japanese shipping has been evident since the beginning of the "China Incident." In the years between 1937 and 1942 the shipping industry applied internal controls, hoping by this method to avoid complete state control. However, since 1942 the Government has strengthened its integrating controls over every aspect of shipping, generally using officials of the more important shipping companies for this purpose. The number of individual companies was reduced, chiefly by mergers, in order to simplify the problems of overall supervision of shipping and to prevent duplication of effort. Ultimately, a single organization dominated by the large operators assumed charge of most phases of commercial marine transportation.

Because of increasing difficulties resulting from bombing and mining of harbors, even more drastic measures have been put into effect. On 1 May 1945, the Government announced the creation of an Inspectorate General of Marine Transportation within the Imperial Headquarters. Joint Army and Navy control was established over both operation and administration of all shipping and port facilities. A few days later Admiral Naokuni Nomura, onetime Navy Minister, was appointed Inspector General and Lt. General Gore Isoya was named chief of staff of the Marine Inspectorate General. The Shipping Headquarters is charged with the actual operation of shipping of the Inspectorate General.

The coordination of shipping control measures in Imperial Headquarters appears to be a logical step at present, in the face of the need for greater integration of all shipping administration. Such measures might seek to cope with underutilization of bottoms and other inefficiencies brought about by private companies seeking their own ends. The progress of bombing operations and the threat of invasion accentuate the problems of making and carrying out quick decisions both nationally and locally. Further reorganization including development of regional controls over all transportation facilities is probable. After years of division of responsibility in the administration of shipping and port facilities, one central headquarters now exists which has control over harbor and warehousing operations and over all merchant vessels whether in the service of the Army and Navy or commercially operated.

Further Deterioration of the Japanese Merchant Shipping Situation

The Japanese merchant shipping situation has now deteriorated to such an extent that it is no longer possible for the Empire to import a sufficient amount of essential commodities even from the near-by areas in northern China and Korea. It is estimated that on 15 July 1945 the total tonnage afloat of Japanese ships over 100 gross tons was about 2,200,000 gross tons (see appendix A, p. 28, below). While it has formerly been customary to compute the damage factor at about 20 percent, it is believed that no accurate computation of damaged Japanese ships can be made at this time, owing to the large number awaiting repair or resting in harbors which have no repair facilities. However, the figure can safely be assumed not to be in excess of 30 percent.

In the fall of 1944 the Japanese had sufficient merchant shipping to supply their home islands with necessary commodities for maintaining their war industries or for supporting further military operations overseas, but not for doing both. The Army-dominated Government decided on the latter course, and convoy after convoy of men and materials was sent to reinforce the garrisons in the Philippines, and imports of raw materials were curtailed. The immediate and obvious effect of such a policy was the sinking of large numbers of these ships, as well as the isolation of others in the southern regions, when the aerial blockade of the South China Sea was established. A more remote effect of this policy has been felt recently in the slowing down of Japan's war industry, including shipbuilding, owing to shortages of critical materials. Thus the shortsightedness of the military rulers of Japan dealt a double blow to their own shipping, enabling the Allies to reduce it substantially.

Even so, new ship construction has enabled the Japanese to maintain their shipping to a certain extent. The standardized shipbuilding program was inaugurated in mid-1943, but the full effects were not felt until 1944. By that time a majority of the principal shipyards, especially those newly established, had devoted their ways to the construction of ships in one or two of the standard sizes, and it is safe to say that practically all of the ships built during 1944–45 have been of the standard types (see appendix B, p. 29, below).

In addition to the standard types of steel ships, wooden cargo vessels of 250, 150, and 100 gross tons have been built as part of the program. While wooden shipbuilding has not reached the proportions anticipated by the Japanese (the current annual production is only about 100,000 gross tons), it is an important factor in coastwise and inter-island shipping and is now being use for overseas traffic as well. As a result of the standardization program, Japanese ship construction during 1944 increased tremendously, and during the latter part of the year more than 120,000 gross tons a month were being completed. This rate declined to about 100,000 gross tons a month during the first quarter of 1945 owing partly to concentration on smaller types of ships and partly to shortages of material and labor. During the second quarter of the year the rate declined still further as a result of the extensive bombing attacks and is at present believed to be no more than 70,000 gross tons a month (see appendix C, p. 30, below). The fitting-out of ships after launching has been especially retarded, indicating that destruction of plants making engines, instruments, and parts affects ship construction as much as direct bombing of shipyards. It is anticipated that this decline will be still further accelerated in the months immediately ahead. It has been reported that tankers under construction have been fitted with cargo hatches and used for dry cargo, and that no further tanker construction is being undertaken.

On the other hand, although the number of sinkings of Japanese ships continues to be high, the average size of ships sunk has decreased markedly, so that the monthly rate of sinkings does not maintain the level reached last winter. This decline can be largely attributed to certain trends which have been particularly noticeable recently. For instance, although the Japanese are known to have a number of large vessels still available (see appendix D, p. 31, below), there appears to be a reliance on smaller ships for the bulk of the shipping between Japan proper and the Asiatic mainland, while many of the larger ones have been observed idle in the ports of the Inland Sea. This allotment probably is an attempt to minimize the targets presented to Allied aircraft, which are now capable of patrolling all the shipping lanes left to the Japanese, and also may be the result of recent mining of Japanese harbors by Allied planes. Furthermore, there has been an almost complete cessation of Japanese shipping between home ports and the southern areas. Although over 10 percent of the remaining tonnage is still in the Netherlands East Indies and Southeast Asia, there has been virtually no effort to move it north for the past 4 or 5 months. It has been reported that some cargoes have been transported north along the China coast to Shanghai in small craft and junks and transshipped from there to Japan in regular cargo vessels, but it is obvious that the volume which can be shipped by such temporary expedients will not be enough to affect the total situation substantially.

Since smaller Japanese ships have taken on added importance, their zone of operation is of considerable interest. The best available figures on their ports of registry were compiled in 1939 (see appendix E, p. 32, below). While the number and use of such ships have changed considerably since that time, it is considered likely that the present distribution of ships in this category will follow approximately the same pattern. Despite the fact that large numbers have been diverted to other areas because of the necessities of war, it is believed that about half of the smaller ships remain close to their home ports. There are also large numbers of small craft still operating in the Netherlands East Indies, but as most of these were seized or built in this territory and are used locally, they do not affect the situation in Japan proper.

While various estimates have been made as to the amount of shipping necessary to maintain the Japanese war economy, it is by now apparent that the tonnage presently available is not sufficient for this purpose, certainly not being enough to allow for any substantial reconstruction of bombed-out plants and urban industrial areas. The Japanese food situation has also been affected by the shortage of ships, and while stockpiles and increased home production may alleviate conditions somewhat, it is clear that there is no permanent solution to the Japanese dilemma.

Japanese Measures against the Allied Threat to Farm Production

Faced with a deteriorating food position in the homeland, the Japanese have been laying special stress upon measures for the protection of crops from Allied air raids and for the increase of farm production. Broadest of these in scope was the proposed establishment of a Farmers Volunteer Corps, the members of which would "plow the fields and cultivate the soil until the very day the enemy should land on our mainland," at which time they would be mobilized and incorporated into the Army. Nearly as broad in scope was the announcement that a plan had been adopted which would guard the fields and crops against Allied chemical warfare. Furthermore, careful instruction was given to farmers on how and when to harvest their wheat in order to foil efforts to burn the crop with incendiary bombs. Finally, in an effort simultaneously to bolster home morale and encourage food production, an organization has been established whose function is to set up shops for manufacturing agricultural tools in the ruins of buildings leveled by air raids. The Japanese predict that during the next 3 months 100,000 pails, hoes, and picks will be manufactured from the metal found in the rubble.

Food Situation in Korea

Korea in normal times supplied a large portion of the food imports into the islands of Japan. However, for the last 2 years, because of poor crops, increased Korean consumption, and transport difficulties, these contributions have been progressively curtailed. The same situation probably will prevail this year because of the poor rice crop last year and the severe cut in the wheat and barley crops of last winter's season. The export of rice from Korea to Japan depends upon an arrangement whereby substitute cereals, notably millet, are imported into Korea from Manchuria.

Lack of a sufficient amount of these imports into Korea, as well as poor crops, has caused a situation that will be very serious for the next 2 or 3 months. The Japanese are concerned about the uneasiness in the farm communities over food supplies. If they cannot correct this situation, then they will, of necessity, start using in Korea the stocks of rice which have been kept for movement to Japan. This in turn will cause serious difficulties in the homeland.

The Food Shortage in Japan

The gradual deterioration in the Japanses food situation which began in 1939–40 has continued at an accelerated rate. Japan is now facing a very serious food shortage in the home islands, a condition which will complicate the problems of Allied occupation authorities. Compared with the national average for the late 1930's, by July of this year the average Japanese caloric consumption had declined 12 percent, while that of nonfarm dwellers, who constitute more than half the population, had fallen 20 percent. The Japanese propaganda machine, which in recent weeks has been overworked with the disquieting theme of food shortages and food substitutes, has admitted that the food situation in Japan does not permit of any optimism.

Decreasing supplies of rice, the basic food of the Japanese, have been the fundamental reason for the present food shortage. According to a Japanese broadcast, the production of rice in 1944 for current consumption is reported to have been 611,290 metric tons less than in 1943. This decrease places the estimated 1944 rice crop at 8,584,000 metric tons. Korea, the most important source of rice imports to Japan, had a very poor rice crop in 1944, with a production of 2,240,000 metric tons in contrast to 2,735,000 metric tons in 1943. To take the place of the rice sent to Japan, Koreans are dependent upon locally produced cereals and those imported from Manchuria. However, the 1945 wheat crop harvest in Korea is unprecedently poor, being only "40 percent of the average year," and there have been difficulties in importing grains from Manchuria for Korea.

It is assumed that a rice stock of about 1 million metric tons was carried over by the Japanese to the current year, as of 1 November 1944. Japan would have, therefore, an extremely small rice supply in the current rice year of about 9,500,000 metric tons, in addition to some small amount of imports. But this estimate does not take into account admittedly serious damage due to air attacks.

In addition to curtailed production, there has been a tendency toward increased consumption of rice by the Japanese. According to an article on 21 December 1944 in *Diayamondo*, an economic magazine published in Tokyo, " . . . efforts are being exerted in cutting down the consumption, but the demands of the whole country still have a tendency to increase. The amount of rice required in military quarters and munition factories must have increased. Because of the system of distribution, those who did not have rice as their staple food are having rice now; so we cannot deny that rice consumption is increasing." The annual utilization of rice by the Japanese in the years from 1938 to 1941 averaged around 11,500, 000 metric tons. Thus there is an apparent shortage at present of 2 million metric tons.

During the past few years, in order to make up this shortage in rice, the Japanese have been dependent upon other grains and foodstuffs to supplement rice in the staple ration. According to a recent Japanese broadcast, however, the national average of wheat and barley crops in 1945 is 73 percent of the crop in 1944, indicating a 1945 crop of only about 2,500,000 metric tons. The ever increasing attention devoted by the Japanese Government to the cultivation of sweet potatoes has had as its object the utilization of sweet potatoes not only for food but also for production of alcohol. The bulk of the production of sweet potatoes in the past has been in the southern part of Japan, especially in the Kagoshima and Okinawa prefectures. The loss of Okinawa may cut Japanese sweet potato production by about 15 percent. Production in Kagoshima may have been seriously affected by the war. In addition, Japanese statements, such as reference to poor weather during planting, lack of seedlings owing to potato spoilage, and the like, are definitely not optimistic. It is believed, therefore, that Japanese production of sweet potatoes in 1945 may be only as much as that in 1944—4,687,000 metric tons, if not less.

In addition to rice, grains, and sweet potatoes, there are requirements for proteins to balance the Japanese diet. Fish supplies, the chief source of animal proteins, are estimated at 1,500,000 metric tons for the total catch in 1944—which is only about half of the 1939 catch. This situation undoubtedly has become more serious in 1945. In order to correct the dietary deficiency, the Japanese authorities have been counting on an increased use of soy beans, much of which is imported from Manchuria.

The principal impact of the over-all food shortage in Japan has fallen upon the industrial cities. In addition, stocks in the cities have been damaged by air attacks, and the dislocation of transportation has complicated the problems of distribution. The situation, as evidenced by the deep concern of the Japanese, is very serious and will become much more critical in the month of September before the new rice harvest can be reaped.

Food Situation in Japan

The Japanese Premier has warned the nation that no early improvement of the food situation could be expected. Nevertheless the following factors may tend to ease the food problem: (1) Japan's fishing fleets, although depleted, will again be able to resume operations and (2) the demobilization of the Army and of war workers will eliminate the extra rations formerly granted those groups, make available additional farm workers, and simplify problems of distribution. Also, the end of the war will make available for human consumption large amounts of agricultural products, particularly sweet potatoes, formerly earmarked for industrial use.[2]

Government Control of Japanese Banks

As the strain upon the Japanese industrial economy has increased, the Government has been forced to tighten its hold upon the nation's financial structure and to take action further ensuring a steady flow of capital and credit to war industries. The munitions companies, especially those of small and medium size, have been in particular need of greater financial support, and this need has been further increased recently as the heavier U. S. air raids have made necessary either extensive repairs or evacuation and dispersal. New regulations, providing greater centralization and increased Government control of the banking system, are largely designed to channel capital and credit directly to these munitions companies. Also, these new measures further implement a long-term program to concentrate and centralize banking institutions, a program which has reduced the number of private commercial banks from 338 in 1939 to between 80 and 90 in 1945.

The most effective of the new regulations is the Emergency Munitions Financing Law, which assigns particular banks to meet the financial needs of specific munitions companies. Rates of interest and conditions of the loans are fixed by the Government. A further provision of the law makes the employees of the designated banks Government employees, thereby strengthening the Government's control of the banks. In order to establish a large pool of capital from which these designated banks can draw, the Government has announced plans for establishing a Government-controlled United Funds Bank. This gigantic institution, having as stockholders 23 of the largest banks in Japan, will make loans to "munitions financing institutions" and to "organizations which undertake work for the national benefit."

Freezing of War Workers on Jobs in Japan

On 26 May the Japanese promulgated a "Law Pertaining to Acutely Vital Affairs of Wartime-essential Personnel." This is a drastic and sweeping move admittedly designed to keep the Japanese, both employers and laborers, on their jobs in essential war industries and on distributing them as the authorities wish. It provides that employers must take the lead in giving the direction to the laborers and in devising remedial measures in case of air raids. Employers cannot leave the sites of their factories or their residences without the permission of the Government officer in charge. In case factories are damaged by air raids, employees must report to that spot or to some place designated by their employers. They must receive the permission of their employers before they leave their places of residence. The members of the Labor Patriotic Service Association, into which many students have been drafted, must abide by the same regulations, taking orders from their group leaders. Independent workers are to consider as their employers the police chiefs or others designated by the local prefectural governors. This tight clamp on all those who were registered for essential war production is a striking example of the difficulties caused to the Japanese economy by air attacks on Japanese industrialized urban areas.

Inflation in Japan

The Japanese Finance Minister, Touosaku Hirose, has warned the Japanese people of impending inflation. Recent Japanese broadcasts have reported that expenditures for defense and payments made on war insurance had raised the total of Bank of Japan notes outstanding to 26 billion yen by the end of June, in contrast to a total of 20 billion yen at the end of March. In January 1943 it stood at 7 billion yen. According to the broadcasts, Hirose "frankly" discussed the question of inflation at a lengthy press conference given by him on 20 July after a Cabinet meeting at which he made a detailed report on the "expanding condition" of Japan's currency. To the press Hirose is reported to have said that "the bubble of inflation in our country is about to burst."

Hirose further stated that "careless expenditures made on capital funds are the root of inflation" and admitted that the "present inflationary tendency is primarily attributable to enormous Government expenditures." Actually the increase in bank notes probably also reflects increased cost of war production, the tendency on the part of real or potential air-raid victims to hoard notes, and, to a lesser extent, black-market operations in Japan.

The countermeasures suggested by the Finance Minister are (1) economy in Government expenditures, (2) stricter control of the distribution of daily necessities, (3) a review of the present policy on foodstuff prices, (4) control of industrial capital, and (5) increased indirect taxes. Japan has not been depending upon taxation as her major source of national revenue. In 1944 taxation covered only 27 percent of the budgetary expenditure. The rest came from borrowing (53 percent) and "other" sources (20 percent), including funds contributed by or seized in the conquered areas.

Reports from neutral observers returning from Japan and Japanese broadcasts have for some time stressed a growing tendency toward inflation in Japan. The Finance Ministry has reached the conclusion "that if such a situation remains unchanged. it will greatly affect the foundation of the Japanese fighting strength." It is believed that Hirose's statements are not merely those of an alarmist but reflect the realization of the Japanese Government that the danger of inflation in Japan is real and imminent.

Japanese Legislation—The Wartime Emergency Measures Bill

The Wartime Emergency Measures Bill approved by the Japanese Diet on 12 June indicates that the Suzuki Government, whatever its ultimate intentions concerning a negotiated peace, is at the moment making detailed plans for a "fight to the last" in the home islands even after central control has broken down. The Bill, which the Japanese themselves described as "most important among the bills introduced before the 87th extraordinary session of the Imperial Diet," makes possible a decentralization of the governmental authority. In the event of a breakdown of communications through invasion or enemy action, each of the eight administrative regions of Japan proper could become autonomous. Up to the present, Japan's wartime controls under the revised National General Mobilization Law of 1941 could be implemented only through decrees from the Emperor. The new Bill, superseding this law, provides that such controls can be enforced not only by Imperial decrees, but also by orders from Ministers in the National Government or from Regional Administrations. Justice Minister Matsuzaka explained that this will permit each regional government to "exercise its own initiative in applying whatever is best suited for that region."

Premier Suzuki, in his address to the Diet which approved the Bill, spoke openly of a possible invasion, declaring, "We will have all the advantages of geography and the solidarity of our people." Later in his address, Suzuki, intending perhaps to inform the Diet that his Cabinet sees no possibility for a negotiated peace at the present time, said, "Judging from the trends within enemy countries and considering the developments in the international situation, I cannot help feel strongly that the only way for us to do is to fight to the last." Even though this declaration may be in part a propagandistic maneuver calculated to elicit negotiation proposals, the provisions of the new Bill indicate that the Government is currently laying plans for a last-ditch fight if no such proposals are forthcoming.

Regional Administration in Japan

With the passage of the Extraordinary War Measures Bill on 12 June the Japanese Diet surrendered its powers for the duration of the war to the Government. All that remains of the Diet is an Extraordinary War Measures Committee to be composed of from 20 to 50 Diet members whom, according to the revised Article 4, the Government "should consult" in exercising its totalitarian powers under the Bill. However, in case of emergency the Government need only to "report" to the Committee after measures are taken.

There is a close connection between the Extraordinary War Measures Bill and the reorganization of the eight regional administrative structures which was announced on 10 June. In the Bill the term "Government" is defined to include the Superintendents-General who will head up the reorganized regional administration. The former Regional Administration Councils and Munitions Superintendence Offices were abolished. In the place of the latter Munitions Supervisory Bureaus are to be established under the Superintendents General. The present reorganization speeds up the process of decentralization with the avowed object of achieving regional administrative autonomy accompanied by economic self-sufficiency to strengthen the defenses of the country. On 19 June, a meeting of the newly appointed Superintendents-General with the Cabinet was held to work out the transfer of powers, the maintenance of liaison, and the operation of a councilor system.

Under the Bill each regional administration is empowered, in case of emergency, to act independently of administrations in other regions and of the central government. The broad scope of this power is stated in Article 1 of the Bill, ". . . the Government [or the Superintendents-General], when urgently necessary, will take steps for the proper measures regardless of the stipulations in other laws and regulations concerning: (1) increase of military and war requirement production; (2) maintenance of the supply of foodstuffs and other requisites of livelihood; (3) maintenance and improvement of transportation and communications; (4) strengthening of defense and maintenance of order; (5) adjustment of the taxation system; (6) measures for war damages; (7) other matters necessary for compensating and manifesting the fighting strength specified by Imperial ordinances."

Since the end of last year there has been a marked trend to decentralize administration and center it in eight districts. As shown in the following table, the districts coincide with the six army districts except that the Central Army district includes three administrative regions.

Army districts	Regional administrative districts	Location of regional superintendents-general offices
Northern	Hokkaido	Sapporo.
Tohoku	Tohoku	Sendai.
Eastern	Kanto-Shinetsu	Tokyo.
Tokai	Tokai-Hokuriku	Nagoya.
Central	Kinki	Osaka.
Central	Chugoku	Hiroshima.
Central	Shikoku	Takamatsu.
Western	Kyushu	Fukuoka.

Additional Regional Administration Organizations in Japan

The trend toward administrative regionalization in Japan continues. The central army district has been subdivided in order to coincide with the three new administrative districts. The Navy has created five new commands so that there may be eight naval commands to correspond with the administrative districts. The banks and large Japanese concerns—Mitsui, Mitsubishi, Sumitomo, and others—are taking similar steps for regional administration. For decades Japanese administration has been centralized in Tokyo. The present regional decentralization is occasioned not only by the fear that the transportation and communication links within Japan may be destroyed, but that Tokyo, the nerve center, may be made completely ineffective.

Evacuation Measures in Japan

As U. S. air raids have increased in volume and in number, with Japanese propagandists declaring that Tokyo has been "literally scorched to the ground," the Japanese have tended to solve their air-raid precaution problems primarily through evacuation and decentralization. A year ago, when maintenance of the dispersal program apparently required an acceleration of the departure of nonessential personnel from the target areas, Japanese authorities were assuring the people that "evacuation is not avoiding the war but taking a battle station." Now indications are that numbers of both essential and nonessential personnel are voluntarily evacuating. To control this exodus, to ensure the evacuation of the nonessential, and to restrain the departure of the essential, the Japanese Government has already enacted some "emergency measures." Further steps probably will be taken soon, and the entire program may then be put on a compulsory basis.

In informing the Japanese people of dispersal plans a year ago, the Government announced that the following 13 cities were to be evacuated: Tokyo, Yokohama, Kawasaki, Yokosuka, Osaka, Kobe, Amagasaki, Nagoya, Moji, Kokura, Tobata, Wakamatsu, and Yawata. Within these designated cities the schools, neighborhood control organizations, public institutions, and certain industrial plants were to be dispersed. In Tokyo itself plans of May 1944 called for the decentralization of the municipal offices, hospitals, schools, and banking companies, excluding those connected with munitions companies and also excluding the control organizations. More recently the Government has undertaken the "dispersal" of dwellings in order to form firebreaks within Tokyo. Several hundred thousand houses have been torn down in creating 100 broad lanes, some of which are more than 600 feet wide. The areas around railroad stations, factories, and traffic centers also were reported as cleared in this fashion.

Personnel designated for evacuation from the 13 named cities included school children and nonessential adults. Approximately 400,-

000 national school children were reported to have been sent with their teachers to rural districts. Adults designated for evacuation were of two classes: (1) those who were personnel of dispersed buildings and organizations and (2) those who were under no necessity to live in dispersed areas. In the second group were named specifically those people whose place of work was outside the designated areas, those whose source of income was outside the areas, and those whose heads of family were not in the areas. More recently, increased emphasis has been placed upon the removal of the aged, infants, and invalids, and on 7 May plans for a "mass evacuation" of nursing babies and expectant mothers were announced.

The designation of personnel considered too essential for evacuation was first made in February of this year. These groups include national and prefectural Government employees, those connected with the production of munitions and daily necessities, members of the medical profession, employees of water and gas companies, employees of banking companies, and newspaper reporters. Older students, held to be vital in part-time production jobs, were added to this list on 31 March. The Japanese population has been evacuated to the country according to a plan prescribing certain rural areas for certain cities. People residing in the Tokyo-Yokohama area have been sent to the Hokkaido, Tohoku, Kanto, and Shinetsu districts; those from Nagoya have been sent to the Tokai and Hokuriku districts and to certain sections of the Kanto and Shinetsu districts; those from the Osaka-Kobe area have been sent to the Kinki and Chugoku districts and to certain localities of the Tokai and Hokuriku districts. Upon their arrival in these rural areas the evacuees are quartered in temples, national schools, and barracks, but plans for "simple homes" have been announced for the future.

In order to utilize this evacuee manpower, the Koiso Cabinet on 30 March adopted an extensive agricultural program through which former forest land, mountain slopes, abandoned factory sites, and other areas not yet fully developed will be cleared and made arable. To prepare the evacuated people for intensive cultivation of the reclaimed land, "mass training" in the raising of potatoes, grains, vegetables, chickens, and rabbits was to be instituted. Besides farm work, the evacuees were to be assigned tasks connected with charcoal-making and pine-root oil extraction.

Japanese announcements of the number of persons evacuated have been contradictory. On 20 April just over 20 percent of the Tokyo populace was said to have been removed. On the following day, however, it was announced that less than 4 million of the city's approximately 7 million still remained. Whatever the extent of evacuation thus far, developments make it clear that the Japanese population recently has been evacuating the cities at an accelerating rate. On 15 March the Government warned the people that an "unsatisfactory response" to the prevailing voluntary system of dispersal would necessitate "appropriate steps." On 4 May, however, an announcement was made of "powerful emergency measures to drive home the meaning of evacuation" and to place "restraint" upon the "general evacuation" from vital cities and from Government and public offices. On 24 May, in a report on the problems that dispersal had brought to savings banks, the Japanese declared that "the population of large cities are showing extreme tendencies toward scattering." This evidence strongly suggests that Japanese evacuation is getting beyond the control of the present semi-voluntary system. As a result, much sterner measures of control can be expected in the near future.

Signs of Deterioration in Japanese Military Morale

The will of Japanese soldiers to resist and their disinclination to surrender, even under the most adverse circumstances, continue to be strong. Over the period from October 1944 through April 1945 only 9 Japanese prisoners of war were taken for every 1,000 reported killed in the Southwest Pacific area, and only 16 were taken for every 1,000 reported killed in Burma. Detailed analysis of available data indicates, however, that there is a measurable deterioration in morale during the progression of each campaign.

Several other types of evidence also indicate that Japanese military morale, while still very high as measured against any general standard, has deteriorated to some extent from previous Japanese standards. These generalizations, however, refer primarily to the final phases of campaigns fought far from Japan in territories where the local populations, for the most part, were friendly to the Allies. The principal evidence from these campaigns is as follows:

(1) An increase in the proportion of deliberate surrender among those captured. (In the Luzon campaign, 14 percent of all prisoners taken up to 21 March 1945 had surrendered deliberately.)

(2) An increase in the proportion of able-bodied personnel among prisoners not known to have surrendered deliberately.

(3) Surrender on the part of commissioned officers.

(4) A small number of surrenders by officer-led groups.

(5) Statements by prisoners indicating deterioration in the morale of units.

(6) Indications during interrogations of prisoners that a changed attitude toward the disgrace of being captured is gaining currency among Japanese troops.

(7) Official concern over desertion and surrender shown in captured Japanese documents.

The intelligence for a detailed study of the Iwo Jima and Okinawa operations is not yet at hand. Preliminary reports indicate little or no weakness in morale in those areas.

In the light of available evidence, an estimate of the over-all situation with respect to Japanese morale permits certain conclusions to be drawn. The force of Allied military operations and increasing Japanese realization of the inadequacy of "spiritual superiority" in the face of shortage of matériel have brought about a condition in which the Japanese do not fight quite so hard at the end of a losing campaign as they did in the earlier years of the war. This tendency has been markedly reinforced by more intensive and increasingly skillful psychological warfare. Mopping-up, therefore, is not likely to be so costly in the future as it was in 1943 and 1944. On the other hand, indications in recent campaigns as at Iwo Jima and Okinawa that the Japanese are substituting planned withdrawals for premature banzai charges and are husbanding fighting personnel by discouraging premature suicide of individuals lead to the conclusion that the middle stages of future campaigns will be prolonged and thus more costly. This view probably needs correction, however, in the light of the well-established fact that Japanese morale is always higher in offensive than in defensive warfare. In a victorious situation Japanese soldiers have a tremendous capacity for intoxicating one another with fanatical fervor. Nevertheless there is abundant evidence that the conviction is beginning to spread among Japanese troops everywhere not merely that particular territories are irrevocably lost, but also that the whole war is lost.

Japanese Military Manpower Potential for 1945

As of 1 June 1945 it is estimated that Japan proper had approximately 10,600,000 men between 17 and 44 years of age still remaining in civil life. Japan's armed forces on the same date were estimated at about 4,800,000 divided approximately as follows: Army Ground Forces, 3,700,000; Army Air Forces, 350,000; and Navy, 750,000. Of the estimated 10,600,000 still in civil life, it is believed that 83 percent are fit for some form of military service (approximately 6,000,000 for general service and 2,800,000 for limited service).

In the past this reserve of Japanese manpower has been used in essential industry and agriculture. Although agricultural requirements continue, the reduction of Japan's economic activity by aerial bombing and blockade has resulted in the release of many workers. Many of these will be needed in civil defense activities (fighting fires, clearing bombed areas, etc.), but after this need has been met, there should still remain a surplus pool of 1,000,000 workers released in the following ways:

(1) There is considerable evidence indicating that a shortage of imported coal and iron has sharply curtailed steel manufacture—a circumstance which would substantially reduce the number of workers required in heavy industry.

(2) On 30 May the Tokyo radio quoted the Minister of Agriculture and Commerce as stating that there was a "noticeable" surplus of factory workers, "especially since the intensification of enemy air raids," and that certain categories of industrial workers who had originally been farmers would be sent back to resume farming activities.[1]

In addition, there will be a considerable number of new workers recruited if replacements are deemed necessary. The natural growth of the population, the continued mobilization of women and school children, and the return of men invalided out of the armed forces

[1] Agriculture and air defense (including the dispersal of plant facilities) are probably the only major Japanese civilian activities which will require an increase in manpower during 1945.

should furnish more than 1,000,000 new workers. Also, it seems clear that other factors will so reduce Japan's industrial activity in 1945 that many workers will be released.

Because of the disruptive effects of air attacks and the necessity of dispersing her industries, Japan may run into serious local labor shortages, particularly in the skilled labor classifications. Nevertheless, it seems fairly clear that the transfer of as many as 2,000,000 men from the working population to the armed forces would not of itself be a limiting factor on Japan's economic activity in 1945.

Estimated Military Use of Manpower Potential

It is not known how many of the estimated 2,000,000 men will be inducted into the armed forces during 1945. The induction of the total number would result in a phenomenal increase—more than 50 per cent of the Army Ground Forces at the beginning of the year. It is estimated that already in 1945—that is, from the beginning of the military year on 1 December 1944 through 1 June 1945—about 700,000 men have been inducted from the double call-up of those who had become 19 or 20 years of age by 1 December 1944. For the remaining 7 months of 1945, therefore, there still remain about 1,300,000 men above economic requirements who are available for induction.

Regular military conscription will continue to supply men to depot divisions at a monthly rate of about 100,000, or even more, while the more flexible system of defense call-up (*Boei Shoshu*) probably will be used to provide personnel for home guard units. That call-up, under the direct control of the Army, will furnish the backbone if not the whole body of the home guard's combat troops. It is not yet known exactly what role the newly formed Civilian Volunteer Corps will play in defense.

In the light of previous practice, it is believed that induction into the armed forces during the remainder of 1945 will conform roughly to the pattern indicated below.

Regular Military Conscription

An estimated 300,000 to 400,000 will be called up from various reserve components (First Reserve, Conscript Reserve, First and Second National Armies), and about the same number from the new

1945 class (19 years old by 1 December 1945) which is due for induction from 1 December 1945 but which may be called earlier. There is also a possibility that some of the current 17- and 18-year olds (that is, those 17 or 18 by 1 December 1945) will be called, as needed, by regular conscription for the formation of new units. In certain strategic areas—Ryukyus, Kuriles, Izus, Bonins, China, and Formosa—they have already been placed under the direct control of the local regimental commander, but men of these ages apparently are used locally, and the military service law still provides that 19 is the minimum age for regular conscription into active service.

Since most of the men now being inducted into the Japanese armed forces are active service conscripts with no previous training, there is usually a time lag of at least 3 months before they are considered available for the formation of new units. By the end of 1945 all of the estimated 700,000 men inducted from 1 December 1944 to 1 June 1945, together with an estimated 400,000 of those still to be inducted, should be trained and ready for use by the armed forces.

Defense Call-up

It is believed that there will be a continued, and perhaps accelerated, call-up of reservists (*Zaigo Gunjin*), which now includes the 17- and 18-year olds of the Second National Army, for home defense in the areas where they reside at present. Such reservists, when called, are attached to regular units (especially antiaircraft) and trained in defense duties. Others are alerted to be called up when invasion is imminent. When called, they are to be formed into independent companies and attached to regular units for the purpose of constructing defense fortifications and, in emergency, engaging in combat. All defense conscripts are expected, however, to engage in regular civilian production as long as possible.

Since the essential purpose of this call-up of reservists is for local defense and since control is in the hands of the commander of the regimental district, the present location of manpower reserves in this category assumes particular importance. All reservists—practically speaking, all fit males 17 to 44—are subject to defense call-up, but it is believed that even those to be called up will be kept in civilian activities as long as possible and, except in extreme emergencies, will not be moved far from their present residences.

In round numbers the estimated number of males 7 to 44 in civilian life as of 1 June 1945 in each of the eight new Army districts is as follows:

Northern	494, 000
Northeastern	928, 000
Eastern	3, 265, 000
East Central	1, 260, 000
Central	2, 060, 000
West Central	773, 000
Shikoku	410, 000
Western	1, 410, 000
Total in Japan proper	10, 600, 000

CHAPTER V

JAPAN'S DEFEAT IN AUGUST 1945

In the first days of August 1945 the Japanese faced the probability of surrender.[11] Ever since the German surrender in May 8, 1945 there had been rumors "that Japan is seeking a negotiated peace." These "unverified reports" were noted in a short article on Japanese Peace Rumors in the Weekly Summary, #125, 31 May 1945. This is reproduced at the end of this chapter. The article discusses "the flood of Japanese propaganda about peace negotiations" and the role of the Soviet Union "as a possible mediator in future negotiations." It is concluded that "none of the reports of Japanese peace feelers thus far has suggested concessions consonant with Japan's present military peril."

Despite the economic collapse of Japan taking place in the spring and summer of 1945, Japan still had a will to resist. The Potsdam Proclamation of July 26, 1945 made by the United States, China and Great Britain had little immediate response.[12] Allied leaders had hoped that it would have had a major impact. The Weekly Summary, #134, 2 August 1945 quoted Premier Suzuki as saying: "As for the Government (of Japan) it does not find any important value in it (the Potsdam Proclamation), and there is no other recourse but to ignore it entirely and resolutely fight for the successful conclusion of this war." The verb "to ignore" is the Japanese word Mokusatsu which might have been translated differently to mean "To delay for a time."[13] This nuance was not noted in the Weekly Summary, for the Joint Intelligence Staff were not linguists. The Weekly Summary optimistically noted that "At any rate, the flat refusal of the Suzuki Government to consider the Potsdam Proclamation would not entirely destroy the effectiveness of that pronouncement as an instrument for undermining the Japanese will to resist to the last man."

The Weekly Summary of 9 August 1945 led off with the statement that "the dropping of the atomic bomb on Hiroshima on August 6 and the declaration of war by the Soviet Union as of 9 August dealt Japan two demoralizing blows in quick succession." President Truman's statement that the atomic bomb was designed to "spare the Japanese people from utter destruction" was noted. The Weekly Summary made an interesting comparison of areas devastated. Air photos had shown that 4.1 square miles of Hiroshima, 60 percent of the city's built-up area had been completely destroyed by the single bomb. In contrast, during the record efforts of the month of July, 4,346 B-29's dropped 32,427 tons of incendiaries on 35 Japanese urban industrial areas, destroying or seriously damaging 29.1 square miles. The Weekly Summary noted some of the initial Japanese broadcasts about the atomic bomb. It concluded its article with these words which were somewhat prophetic: "It is clear, however, that the bomb (and the scientific development behind it) as both a psychological and a military weapon will have an incalculable effect upon present and future warfare."

The coupling of the atomic bombing and the Soviet Union's entry into the war in the Weekly Summary is rather interesting. To some Japanese leaders the Russian entry was more of a shock than the explosion of the atomic bomb, a weapon they could not comprehend. They had hoped that the Soviet Union would act as an intermediary in peace negotiations. Actually, the Russians entered into the war because they expected an immediate Japanese surrender and they wished to be on the side of the victorious Allies.[14]

The United States had been urging the entry of the Soviet Union into the war for many months. At the Yalta Conference in February of 1945 various promises for post-war settlement of territorial claims and zones of influence had been made to Joseph Stalin by President Roosevelt. The main reason that the United States so ardently wished a Soviet attack was the existence of the vaunted Kwantung Army of the Japanese in Manchuria. The Weekly Summary of 31 May 1945 in a short article noted that the Kwantung Army was "one of the most powerful sections of the Japanese military machine" and had "dominated the political, economic, and military administration of Manchuria since 1931." The Kwantung Army was thought to have a core of some 700,000 Japanese soldiers, plus some 300,000 Manchurian troops. It was a formidable force which would be on the flank of the American troops when they made landings in Kyushu. American strategic planners were anxious to have Soviet forces engage the Kwantung Army. Actually, it developed that this army was not so powerful as it had seemed. The United States need not have been so insistent on the Soviet Union's entry into the war.[15]

With the dropping of the second atomic bomb on Nagasaki on August 9, the Japanese offer to end the war on August 10 and the Japanese acceptance of unconditional surrender on August 14, the Pacific War was ended on August 15. The difficult task of accepting the surrender of 5.3 million Japanese armed forces in addition to 950,000 Chinese puppet troops and 300,000 Manchurian troops was staggering. The surrender may have been made easier for some

Japanese by the historic radio broadcast of the Emperor of Japan on August 14.[16] It is noted in the Weekly Summary that the Emperor had said that "he had accepted the Potsdam ultimatum to avoid the possible extermination of the Japanese race and of all humanity by the atomic bomb." The Emperor bade his subjects to "work with resolution" and "to keep pace with the progress of the world." The Chief of the Overseas Bureau of the Japanese Broadcasting System gave a statement of unrepentant nationalism which was quoted in the Weekly Summary: "We did not lose because we were wrong or our thoughts were erroneous. It is because we lacked the material strength; we lacked the necessary scientific knowledge and equipment, so this mistake of ours we must amend. As a race we are still strong." This emphasis upon scientific knowledge and equipment is interesting reading today.

After the shock of surrender some considered views of Japan's war economy were noted in the Weekly Summary of 30 August 1945. A frank analysis in the Asahi newspaper "concluded that Japan's economic ability to continue the war was lost long before the appearance of the atomic bomb and the Soviet declaration of war." The newspaper account stressed that "after the loss of Okinawa the building up of an economic unit of Japan, Manchuria and China became a hopeless task. Thus, Japan had no alternative but to rely upon the homeland which, however, was subjected to intensified strategic bombing by B-29's." Moreover, according to the Asahi, "The air defense of war plants, the evacuation of munitions factories, and the installations of underground facilities failed to keep pace with U.S. air attacks. The attacks on secondary cities caused great damage to the small workshops, which were an integral part of the war economy. Therefore, Japan had an inadequate economic base for the continuation of hostilities."

All during the Pacific War there was a deep concern within the intelligence community for information on the Japanese activities in those areas which Japan had conquered. With the economic collapse of Japan and its military surrender, the acceptance of the surrender of Japanese troops was a stupendous task in those areas. The Weekly Summary, #136, 16 August 1945, carried a lengthy article on The Failure of the Greater East Asia Co-Prosperity Sphere. It is noted that though Japan's military defeat caused the failure of GEA, "There is a possibility that a similar plan for a Pan-Asia will emerge in the future."

Since the final collapse of Germany there have been a number of unverified reports that Japan is seeking a negotiated peace. Although some of these reports are alleged to have emanated from Japanese diplomats in Europe, no serious Japanese Government bid for peace has yet emerged. Japanese official propagandists have issued a steady series of denials of any efforts to negotiate peace, but their number and the equivocal phrasing of some of them indicate the possibility that the denials themselves are virtual peace feelers. Given the present seriousness of the military situation and the character of the Suzuki Government, the flood of rumors and open discussion of them suggest that a negotiated peace may be the ultimate goal of Japan's leaders.

The composition and character of the present Japanese Government probably is the most positive factor in the possibility of a peace by negotiation. Premier Suzuki has gathered about him a group of elder statesmen representing a wide range of national interests and could attempt peace negotiations without particularly discrediting or committing the military. However, the military appears still to retain a major share of the power behind the facade of the nonmilitary Cabinet members, and in the end the negotiators would have to depend upon the military to carry out the peace terms.

Amid the flood of Japanese propaganda about peace negotiations several statements in particular have suggested that the leaders of Japan are carefully scrutinizing U. S. public utterances for possible peace offers. In reply to President Truman's declaration that U. S. war aims do not include the extermination of the Japanese people, radio Tokyo said, "The U. S. Government must give proof to the President's proclamation through action and not merely through words." Concurrently the Soviet Union has been mentioned repeatedly as a possible mediator in future negotiations. The most overt of these suggestions was made on 25 May over radio

Tokyo: while "answering" rumors that Japan hopes to get the U. S. S. R. to mediate, a commentator conceded that "if Japan wished to make peace, it would be conceivable for her to make peace proposals by way of the Soviet Union—a possibility which we are quite ready to admit."

From the Japanese point of view the outlook for a negotiated peace probably does not appear hopeless. The U. S. proposals of 25 November 1941 offered, in essence, liberal terms of economic and political cooperation on condition that Japan abandon the Tripartite Axis Pact and forego aggression. With the collapse of Germany the Pact became extinct, and after promising to abandon their aggressive policy Japanese leaders might offer to accept the U. S. terms of 1941, arguing that continuation of the war had no point other than U.S. vengeance. The Japanese may also believe that the U. S. S. R. is interested in maintaining an independent though insular Japan as a barrier to U. S. power and that the Soviets are interested in denying to the United States the political prestige in Asia that a complete victory would bring.

Whatever the extent of Japanese hopes and desires for ending the war through negotiation instead of utter defeat, none of the reports of Japanese peace feelers thus far has suggested concessions consonant with Japan's present military peril. According to unverified reports, the Japanese have declared themselves willing to withdraw from southeastern Asia and China; to make Manchuria independent or to return it to China, but in either case to retain some economic rights in the area; and to reorganize the present Cabinet with a civilian as Premier. They have also declared that Japan should be allowed to retain the homeland, Formosa, and the Kurile Islands and should be granted the right to conduct foreign trade. Very probably this position is merely the first stage in what may become a lengthy bargaining process, and the Japanese may be willing to pay an increasingly higher price for a peace short of "unconditional surrender" as time goes on.

Japanese Response to the Potsdam Proclamation

The immediate response of the Japanese to the Potsdam Proclamation has been in the negative. Japanese propagandists, in radio and press releases for consumption at home and abroad, have taken the line that the Allied statement of terms for immediate surrender was merely a propaganda measure designed both to bolster morale in the United States and to undermine morale in Japan. In order to illustrate the theme that the average Japanese felt only increased determination after hearing the proclamation, the Tokyo radio broadcast "interviews" in which railway workers, teachers, university students, barbers, and policemen were unanimous in describing the terms as "ridiculous." In an official response, broadcast primarily to listeners outside Japan, Premier Suzuki said of the joint proclamation, "As for the Government, it does not find any important value in it, and there is no other recourse but to ignore it entirely and resolutely fight for the successful conclusion of this war."

Despite these denials of interest in the Potsdam Proclamation, there were indications in Japan last week of some discontent with the present Government's policy. One newspaper vigorously assailed the Suzuki Cabinet, blaming a lack of public support of the Government upon "ineptness in political technique." Another sharply attacked the Suzuki Cabinet's prosecution of the war and demanded that "something be done" about the Allied air raids on medium-sized and smaller cities.

Actually, in order to maintain its prestige in the eyes of the Japanese people, the Suzuki Government would be forced to give the appearance of disregarding the peace terms regardless of its ultimate intentions concerning them. Furthermore, indications of genuine interest would be revealed through diplomatic channels, not through the columns of the press. At any rate, the flat refusal of the Suzuki Government to consider the Potsdam Proclamation would not entirely destroy the effectiveness of that pronouncement as an instrument for undermining the Japanese will to resist to the last man.

WEEKLY SUMMARY

The dropping of the atomic bomb on Hiroshima on 6 August and the declaration of war by the Soviet Union as of 9 August dealt Japan two demoralizing blows in quick succession.

First Use of the Atomic Bomb

President Truman's statement 16 hours after the dropping of the atomic bomb on Hiroshima linked it with the Potsdam ultimatum of 26 July, which was designed to "spare the Japanese people from utter destruction." He said, "If they do not now accept our terms, they may expect a rain of ruin from the air, the like of which has never been seen on this earth."

It has been officially announced that preliminary examination of reconnaissance photographs indicates that 4.1 square miles of Hiroshima—60 percent of the city's built-up area—was completely destroyed by the effect of the bomb. Within the city, 5 major industrial targets were destroyed, and additional damage outside the completely destroyed area was caused. No comparison with previous efforts affords an adequate measure of the effectiveness of this revolutionary instrument of destruction. However, during the record efforts of July, 4,346 B-29s dropped 32,427 tons of incendiaries on 35 Japanese urban industrial areas, destroying or seriously damaging 29.11 square miles. Comparing these figures with the destruction wrought by the atomic bomb, it appears that the destruction is equivalent to that caused by 612 B-29s dropping 4,567 tons of incendiaries. It may also be noted that thus far only one B-29 operation has surpassed in magnitude the theoretical attack used for purposes of comparison.

Serious concern and some signs of panic are evident in Japanese broadcasts. Propagandists have told the people to be careful "not to be deceived by the enemy's strategy" of combining the use of the new bomb with intensified propaganda measures, and there were several indications that a new ultimatum from the Allied leaders was expected in the near future.

Virtually no operational details of the first use of the bomb have been released, other than the fact that the bomb was dropped by a single B–29 in daylight. The Japanese statement that a bomb was dropped by parachute and exploded before it reached the ground has not been officially confirmed. It is clear, however, that the bomb (and the scientific development behind it) as both a psychological and a military weapon will have an incalculable effect upon present and future warfare.

Soviet Declaration of War against Japan

On 2 hours' notice to the Japanese Ambassador in Moscow the Soviet Government announced a state of war existing between Japan and the U. S. S. R. as of 9 August. The Soviet Union based its action upon Japan's failure to accept the Potsdam ultimatum by the United States, Great Britain, and China. The Japanese rejection of the ultimatum, according to the Soviet announcement, made groundless a "Japanese request for Soviet mediation for peace." Consequently the U. S. S. R. stated that it was entering the war to shorten it and give the Japanese people a possibility of avoiding the destruction suffered by the Germans.

Changes in Kwantung Army Control in Manchuria

As war approaches Japan's inner zone and as the maintenance of good relations with the Soviet Union becomes increasingly important to the Japanese, certain administrative changes in Manchuria have been made which tend to augment the influence of the Japanese Foreign Office in that area and to decrease, on the surface at least, the political control of the Kwantung Army. This army, one of the most powerful sections of the Japanese military machine, has dominated the political, economic, and military administration of Manchuria since 1931. Its commander in chief concurrently serves as Ambassador from Japan and as such actually exercises supervisory control over the Manchukuo puppet government. Until recently he also had final jurisdiction over the government of the Kwantung Leased Territory.

By undertaking aggressive action not in line with Japan's prevailing foreign policy, the Kwantung Army has been known to force new departures in Japanese strategy, if not in ultimate objectives. Thus it precipitated the Japanese invasion of Manchuria in 1931. The Japanese Foreign Ministry, though temporarily embarrassed by this action, subsequently endorsed its results.

During the past year several appointments have been made in an apparent effort to forestall any similar independent action of the Kwantung Army which might compromise Japan's relations with the U. S. S. R. In July 1944, General Umezu, known as the "strong man" of the Kwantung Army, was replaced as commander in chief by General Yamada and was promoted to Chief of Staff of the whole Japanese Army. Umezu's promotion, which put a Kwantung Army man in the top military councils of the country, may have been designed to reconcile the policy of the Kwantung Army with the over-all military policy of Japan. More important, Yamada, according to some reports, is more amenable to central Japanese authority than was Umezu and is therefore less likely to take separate action.

In the political sphere the power of the Kwantung Army has been invaded by the dispatch of two prominent Foreign Office men to serve successively as Minister Plenipotentiary to the Manchukuo puppet government. The selection of such influential men as a former Vice Foreign Minister and a director of the Foreign Ministry's Political Affairs Bureau indicates that some of the functions of the Ambassador to Manchukuo have been transferred out of the hands of the Kwantung Army. In April 1945 the Ambassador was also relieved of part of his jurisdiction over the Kwantung Leased Territory, a move which apparently reverses the former Japanese policy of coordinating the administration of Manchukuo and Kwantung.

16 August 1945

WEEKLY SUMMARY

In a note delivered to President Truman at 1810 on 14 August the Japanese Government, in the name of the Emperor, accepted unconditional surrender in accordance with the Potsdam ultimatum and the answer of the Four Powers to the Japanese surrender offer of 10 August. On 10 August the Japanese Government had sent notes to the United States, Great Britain, China, and the U. S. S. R. stating its readiness to end the war on the basis of the Potsdam ultimatum, "with the understanding that the said declaration does not comprise any demand which prejudices the prerogatives of His Majesty as a sovereign ruler." Thereupon the United States, on behalf of the Allies, replied that from the "moment of surrender the authority of the Emperor and the Japanese Government to rule the State shall be subject to the Supreme Commander of the Allied Powers, who will take such steps as he deems proper to effectuate surrender terms. The Emperor will be required to authorize and insure the signature of the Government of Japan and the Japanese Imperial Headquarters of the surrender terms necessary to carry out the provisions of the Potsdam Declaration . . . . The ultimate form of government of Japan shall . . . be established by the freely expressed will of the Japanese people." President Truman, shortly after receiving the Japanese Government's answer of 14 August, announced acceptance of the surrender offer, and a note was given to the Swiss directing the Japanese Government to order prompt cessation of hostilities and to inform General Douglas MacArthur, designated by the Allies to receive the surrender, of the effective date and hour of the termination of hostilities. The Japanese also were ordered to dispatch emissaries at once to General MacArthur, who was empowered to make the necessary arrangements for their arrival at the place designated by him for the formal surrender.

At 2300 on 14 August the Emperor broadcast to home and foreign audiences, declaring that he had accepted the Potsdam ultimatum to avoid possible extermination of the Japanese race and of all humanity by the atomic bomb. An hour later an announcement of the surrender was broadcast to the Japanese armed forces. Subsequently they were officially ordered to cease hostilities, but the Japanese Government has informed General MacArthur that it may require as long as 12 days to communicate this order to all elements. General MacArthur had already issued a warning order for the occupation of Japan and Korea by Allied forces but set no date for landings. Allied commanders are now instructing the Japanese in the procedure to be followed in implementing the capitulation of their armed forces, estimated at approximately 5,300,000, besides about 950,000 Chinese puppet troops and 250,000 Manchukuoan puppets.

Official Japan in Defeat

In the week following the dispatch of the final surrender note to President Truman several aspects of the Japanese state of mind have begun to emerge.[1] Both the actions and statements of the Japanese leaders reveal an underlying mixture of subjection and muted defiance. The leaders of the Japanese Government give evidence of faithfully meeting Allied demands, and the Japanese press has been particularly realistic in describing the surrender. The new Cabinet seems predominately to be a nonmilitary government. The Japanese envoys summoned to Manila to arrange the details of the military surrender worked cooperatively, and the Japanese Government has since announced to its people the scheduled initial Allied landing on 26 August. However, public spokesmen still make assertions of undiminished national pride. Japanese officials have thus far been exceedingly cautious about using the words *surrender* and *defeat* and have sought to give the impression that the capitulation was a voluntary decision taken by the Emperor to insure the welfare of the Japanese people. Furthermore, Japanese spokesmen have been frank in blaming the inferiority of their science, not their international policy, for their present plight.

The new Cabinet was formed by Prince Naruhiko Higashi-Kuni on 16 August. Despite his career as a soldier, the choice of Higashi-Kuni was taken by Japanese propagandists to be in accord with the demands of the Potsdam Declaration for a nonmilitary government. Furthermore, it was stressed that the choice was made entirely upon the Emperor's initiative, without the customary conference with elder statesmen. Aside from Higashi-Kuni, who is War Minister as well as Premier, two other military men were appointed to the Cabinet, including Admiral Mitsumasa Yonai, Minister of the Navy. In his first speech to the Japanese people

Premier Higashi-Kuni declared that as Japan forges ahead, "the entire world will cast eyes of admiration at the greatness of our national policy." In speaking of future relations with foreign countries he mentioned "the liberation of East Asia" and asserted that "in the future we must encourage each other in the development of East Asia. This, I hope, will be able to contribute to world peace."

Tokyo newspapers have labored to bring full realization of Japan's present situation to the people. All newspapers published the Potsdam Declaration and the subsequent Allied and Japanese notes. *Asahi Shimbun* warned them that "what the Japanese nation is confronted with is not negotiated peace, but one-sided defeat." The *Mainichi Shimbun* urged them to remember that "the new bomb constituted only one factor in bringing the war to a disadvantage against Japan and [that] even without the use of the atomic bomb Japan's position was far from satisfactory."

However, the Imperial Rescript announcing the surrender to the Japanese people on 14 August stated somewhat equivocally that despite the gallant efforts, "the war situation has developed not necessarily to Japan's advantage." Moreover, the Allies had begun to use "a new and most cruel bomb", and continued resistance would lead only to "the obliteration of the Japanese nation" and to "the total extinction of human civilization." After expressing his deep regret to "our allied nations of East Asia who have consistently cooperated with the Empire toward the emancipation of East Asia," the Emperor bade his subjects to "work with resolution" and "keep pace with the progress of the world." Premier Suzuki's speech of resignation on the same day was even more outspokenly bitter concerning the atomic bomb, which he termed "a murder weapon." The present concern of the Japanese people, he said without further explanation, is "the national polity. We are very proud of our national polity."

In speaking of the hard future ahead, Suzuki declared, "we must devote our efforts to the improvement of our sciences, which was a lack in this war. In so doing, we must contribute to the world." The most outspoken statement of dogged nationalism was issued by Kusuo Oya, chief of the Overseas Bureau of the Japanese Broadcasting System: "We did not lose because we were wrong or our thoughts were erroneous. It is because we lacked the material strength; we lacked the necessary scientific knowledge and equipment. So this mistake of ours we must amend. As a race we are still strong."

Japanese View of Japan's War Economy

A frank analysis of Japan's war economy was given by the *Asahi Shimbun* on 25 August. It concluded that Japan's economic ability to continue the war was lost long before the appearance of the atomic bomb and the Soviet declaration of war. The article states that in the first few months of the war the strategic resources of the southern regions gave Japan an economic potential to match the United States and Great Britain but that the development of these resources was hampered by the mounting shortage of ships. The shipping losses in one month in 1944, according to *Asahi Shimbun,* was one-half million tons. With the fall of Saipan in July of 1944, Japan was partially cut off from the southern regions, and with the start of U. S. operations in the Philippines the severance was complete.

Thereafter the Japanese laid plans for the development of the resources of the inner zone, but these had small prospects for success in view of mounting difficulties, especially of transportation. After the loss of Okinawa the building up of an economic unit of Japan, Manchuria, and China became a hopeless task.

Thus Japan had no alternative but to rely upon the homeland, which, however, was subjected to intensified strategic bombing by B–29s. Moreover, according to *Asahi Shimbun,* the air defense of war plants, the evacuation of munitions factories, and the installation of underground facilities failed to keep pace with U. S. air attacks. The attacks on secondary industrial cities caused great damage to the small workshops, which were an integral part of the war economy. Therefore, Japan had an inadequate economic base for the continuation of hostilities.

The Failure of the Greater East Asia Co-Prosperity Sphere

Japanese spokesmen have variously described the Greater East Asia Co-Prosperity Sphere (GEA) as "an international order based upon common prosperity" and as a device for "the development of the Japanese race." These expressions of high idealism and frank opportunism represent the range of motivation behind the establishment and administration of the GEA. Japanese scholars, businessmen, and Army leaders have injected into the GEA both the traditional Japanese symbolism of *Hakko Ichiu* ("the eight corners of the world beneath one roof") and the militarists' pragmatic policy of armed expansion. This fusion of motivations has found its fullest expression in the war in the Pacific, which the Japanese have named the "holy war," or the "Greater East Asia War." Through their insistence that Japanese soldiers are fighting for the establishment of a new order in Greater East Asia, the official spokesmen have linked success for the GEA with victory for the Japanese Army. Japan's military defeat necessarily involves the immediate failure of the GEA program, the effectiveness of which already had been limited by the underlying divergence of purpose between its idealistic and opportunistic supporters. If, however, the Japanese have had even fragmentary success in establishing a political, economic, and cultural union in Greater East Asia, and if the people of Asia do not gain security and stability in the postwar settlement, there is a possibility that a similar plan for a Pan-Asia will emerge in the future.

Insofar as it involves continental conquest, the GEA is merely the latest manifestation of the centuries-old Japanese expansionist tradition. In the late nineteenth century Japanese patriotic secret societies were formed in order to promote Japanese expansion and imperialism through mobilizing Japanese finance and trained personnel for espionage and propaganda work in Asia. Early in the twentieth century, greatly under the influence of the secret societies, the expansionist tradition was transformed into the Great Asia doctrine. Although the supporters of this doctrine differed among themselves concerning the nature and the degree of desired Japanese domination in a Pan-Asia, they agreed that European and U. S. interests in the Orient were responsible for reducing Asiatic countries to semi-colonial status. Agreeing upon a theory of regionalism not unlike that underlying the Monroe Doctrine, they created the slogan "Asia for Asiatics." Many aspects of this doctrine were incorporated into the official foreign policy of Japan by the Konoye Cabinet in 1938. The policy was named the "New Order in East Asia." When the fall of France and the Netherlands in 1940 opened to the Japanese the possibility of easy expansion into European holdings in the Orient, this policy was restated as the "New Order in Greater East Asia." Later, in order to incorporate into this policy ideas of economic cooperation in Asia, the title became the "Greater East Asia Co-Prosperity Sphere." In November 1942 the policy was given even fuller sanction when the Greater East Asia Ministry was established and its first minister, Kazuo Aoki, was charged with the administration of political, economic, and cultural affairs in China, Manchuria, Thailand, French Indochina, Burma, the Philippines, and the Celebes.

The establishment of the GEA Ministry was effected by the dominant Army group in a maneuver designed to eclipse the power of the Ministry of Foreign Affairs. In a year of military successes ranging geographically from Kiska to New Guinea, the Japanese Army leaders were confident of successfully completing Japanese expansion in Greater East Asia, and they were impatient of the less militant policies of the career diplomats in the Foreign Affairs Ministry. They appointed Aoki, known to be an Army supporter, an expansionist, and a Greater Japan enthusiast, as GEA Minister. The new ministry was given jurisdiction over matters formerly directed by the Ministry of Foreign Affairs, excepting only "purely diplomatic" concerns. Both the GEA Ministry and the subsequently reorganized Foreign Affairs Ministry were staffed largely by undistinguished bureaucrats who could be counted upon to support the military in establishing a "New Order in Greater East Asia" by conquest.

With the fall of the Tojo Cabinet in July 1944, following a series of U. S. military successes culminating in the capture of bases in the Marianas less than 1,500 miles from Tokyo, the career diplomats of the Foreign Affairs Ministry regained a considerable portion of their lost power and prestige at the expense of an independent GEA administration. Mamoru Shigemitsu, who had served as Minister of Foreign

Affairs in the Tojo Cabinet, was retained in that post in the new Koiso Cabinet and was appointed GEA Minister concurrently. Again in the Suzuki Cabinet, established in March 1945, Shigenori Togo—another career diplomat—was given both posts. The appointment of Togo, who had resigned as Minister of Foreign Affairs in 1942 when the establishment of the GEA Ministry stripped his position of its powers, indicated that the career diplomats had completely regained their former position.

Because of its dominance by Army leadership at the time of its inception, the fundamental aims of the GEA Ministry were to provide ideological support for the conquest of the Asiatic continent and the southern regions and to set up administrative machinery for the conquered areas. Despite this role as an adjunct to conquest, the leaders of the GEA presented their objectives in terms of the highest idealism. Even later, when the ardor of both the militarists and the more moderate GEA idealists had been cooled somewhat by the menace of increased Allied military power, the professions of idealism continued. Many Japanese, both inside the GEA movement and outside it, probably believe sincerely in working toward Asiatic cooperation, equality, and prosperity under benevolent Japanese leadership.

The fullest statement of GEA ideals is the Joint Declaration adopted by the Assembly of Greater East Asiatic Nations in November 1943. This five-point declaration, following a preamble announcing the hope of the countries of Greater East Asia of liberating themselves from "the yoke of British-American domination," reads as follows:

1. The countries of Greater East Asia through mutual cooperation will ensure the stability of their region and construct an order of common prosperity and well-being based upon justice.

2. The countries of Greater East Asia will ensure the fraternity of nations in their region, by respecting one another's sovereignty and independence and practicing mutual assistance and amity.

3. The countries of Greater East Asia, by respecting one another's traditions and developing the creative faculties of each race, will enhance the culture and civilization of Greater East Asia.

4. The countries of Greater East Asia will endeavor to accelerate their economic development through close cooperation upon a basis of reciprocity and to promote thereby the general prosperity of their region.

5. The countries of Greater East Asia will cultivate friendly relations with all the countries of the world and work for the abolition of racial discriminations, the promotion of cultural intercourse, and the opening of resources throughout the world, and contribute thereby to the progress of mankind.

Within the framework of this announcement of intentions, the GEA Ministry set up political, economic, and cultural programs which were designed to secure the maximum cooperation from the conquered populations of Greater East Asia.

The GEA Ministry is organized in accord with the regional theory that supports the entire GEA concept. The Ministry is divided into five bureaus: the Secretariat, the General Affairs Bureau, the Manchurian Affairs Bureau, the China Affairs Bureau, and the Southern Affairs Bureau. Each bureau is charged with the administration in its own region of all GEA functions, which are defined as the execution of political affairs other than purely diplomatic affairs, the protection and supervision of Japanese commerce and Japanese nationals, the supervision of colonization, the administration of colonial enterprises, and the direction of cultural programs. GEA embassies and consulates in the various regions implement the authority of the bureaus.

In establishing the political administration of Greater East Asia the GEA Ministry gave the outward appearance of observing Article 2 of the Joint Declaration, which promised mutual respect of "one another's sovereignty and independence." China, Burma, and the Philippines were "declared independent" by October 1943, and puppet governments were established. French Indochina was "declared an autonomous province." To present the appearance of respecting the political autonomy of those regions where "independence" was not granted, the GEA Ministry made a point of appointing a number of native administrators. In Java, for example, several native officials were made mayors of their municipalities. Also, the Ministry established institutes both in Japan and in the GEA areas for training natives to be "leaders of their people." Behind this facade of autonomy and independence, however, the GEA Ministry has steadily maintained firm control of the political administration of the regions under its jurisdiction. The puppet regimes of China, Burma, and the Philippines were amenable to this control because of their dependence upon the Japanese Army for their security. The GEA Ministry in 1942 dispatched approximately 100,000 Japanese government officials to the southern regions to administer local governments. Furthermore, a number of institutes were created for the purpose of training Japanese officials "to direct local inhabitants." Somewhat less directly, Japanese already living in the southern regions were indoctrinated with the necessity for gaining the confidence and respect of the native populations. Finally, political associations modeled upon the Japanese pattern, such as the East Asia Assistance Association in northern China, were established to aid in maintaining political control of the GEA areas.

Article 4 of the Joint Declaration promised that the nations of the GEA would "endeavor to accelerate their economic development through close cooperation upon a basis of reciprocity." The GEA Ministry interpreted this article to mean that the economy of the GEA should be centralized under the control of the Japanese. Accordingly, plans were made to divide the GEA into three industrial zones. The central, or chief, zone, comprising the Japanese home islands, was planned to engage in the manufacture of light machinery, precision instruments, chemical production, and the bulk of heavy industrial production. The second zone, including China and Manchuria, was to engage in certain heavy industries, mining, light metal production, and the production of power. The third zone, including all of the occupied territory of Southeast Asia, was primarily to deliver raw materials to the industrial areas but was to be permitted to engage in such manufacture as would benefit from proximity to raw materials, such as crude-iron and aluminum production. More recently, with the impossibility of full movement of commodities, the policy of economic self-sufficiency was introduced for the southern regions. Fiscal policy was to make the Japanese yen the standard of all GEA currencies and the basis for all financial transactions. Under the direction of the GEA Ministry Japanese banks established over 200 branches in the southern regions, and 60 percent of all bank deposits in the area were deposited in Japanese-owned banks. Furthermore, the Special Wartime Corporation was established to finance and control the development of resources in the Philippines, Malaya, Borneo, the Celebes, eastern French Indochina, and Burma.

The cultural program of the GEA Ministry has been diversified and energetic. Although lip service was paid to the policy of respecting the various cultures of the GEA, in actual practice the Ministry worked steadily to impose a considerable degree of Japanese culture upon the other members of the GEA. From the very beginning strenuous efforts were made to establish Japanese as the official language of the GEA. Large numbers of Japanese school teachers were sent overseas "to educate the younger generations of the southern regions through the guidance of Japanese culture." The GEA Ministry also arranged for the education in Japan of college and university students from the GEA. It was estimated in September 1943 that there were 3,000 such students in Japan. At the same time the purpose of this educational program was made clear by the statement that in obtaining future foreign students "excellence in scholarship is important, but selection must also depend upon the suitability of the students to become leaders in the construction of the GEA."

In addition to formal classroom teaching, the GEA Ministry instituted a highly diversified program of cultural instruction. Cultural "institutes" and cultural "museums"—some of them, such as the one in Bangkok, luxurious and elaborate—were established for the purpose of displaying "correct" Japanese culture through exhibits, lectures, and motion pictures. Cultural "missions" made up of representatives from the GEA countries made 3-month tours of investigation in Japan. *A History of Greater East Asia*, a thousand-page volume requiring 2 years to write and edit, undertook to clarify "the position of Japan as leader of the GEA." Annual GEA Literary Conferences were held with the announced purpose of considering "practical" means for blotting out the influence of Anglo-American culture in East Asia. A GEA Musical Association, indicating the political possibilities of the cultural program, sponsored two new musical compositions "The Burma Independence March," and "The Philippines Independence March."

The religious policy of the GEA Ministry was "to recognize all regions of Southeast Asia as they are, for the time being at least, and give them every possible aid and protection, while exercising constant efforts to guide them along a healthy path step by step." The goal to which this "healthy path" was to lead, according to one spokesman, was a common GEA "primitive religion" which would embrace Shintoism. For the benefit of the Buddhists in the GEA, the Japanese have emphasized that Buddhism is widely practiced in Japan. An East Asia Buddhist Research Institute was established in Tokyo and missions were sent abroad "to study the affairs of Buddhism in all parts of the GEA." The nonreligious aspects of these missions were emphasized by the announcement that one mission was to spend a year in Burma, Thailand, and the southern regions "to increase amity and cooperation among the natives."

The racial policy of the GEA Ministry was based upon the portion of Article 5 of the Joint Declaration which called for "the abolition of racial discriminations." The Ministry announced that this was to be "not mere mechanical equality" but a plan enabling "all peoples to live in contentment and peace." The dynamic idea expressed in this statement of intention, however, was put into practice on a relatively small scale. In Shanghai the foreign YMCA, formerly closed to Japanese and Chinese, was renamed "The GEA Home" and opened to "all GEA peoples." But the policy remained implicit in the entire GEA program aimed at "liberating the region from the yoke of British-American domination."

Despite the grandeur of the vision of a GEA, the popular appeal of the slogan "Asia for Asiatics," and the energy and diversity with which the Japanese have sought to establish the GEA, the plan for joining nearly 1 billion people into a political, economic, and cultural union has been a failure. The most obvious source of this failure has been the decline and final collapse of Japanese military fortunes. The necessity for fighting a bitter hemispheric war while attempting to establish the Pan-Asiatic ideal has been an impossible handicap for the Japanese. Military security prevented them from permitting any genuine autonomy among native populations; military necessity prohibited the establishment of any genuine economic reciprocity; military urgency interfered with their attempts to attain cultural understanding with the peoples of the GEA.

Another source of failure perhaps equally important was the lack of a unified motivation behind the GEA Ministry. The Ministry was dominated from its inception by Army leaders determined to exploit the ideology of Pan-Asia for immediate advantages. Its policy was inevitably two-sided. This dichotomy of purpose was perhaps reflected in the behavior of Japanese businessmen overseas who, despite the cautions of the GEA Ministry to be careful in their treatment of the people with whom they lived, saw in the GEA only an opportunity for economic exploitation. Also, despite their indoctrination, Japanese officials sent to administer GEA regions displayed a tendency to disregard the sensibilities of native peoples. Repeated warnings were sent out to these officials "not to show superiority even when they know they are superior." Japanese soldiers were even worse offenders in this respect and won a particularly bad reputation in Burma, where they desecrated religious shrines and mistreated Burmese ecclesiastics. Part of this misbehavior may be attributed to the inability of the average Japanese to perform the intellectual jugglery necessary to see that in conquering vast portions of the Asiatic continent and the South Seas he was fighting "a holy war" and establishing "an order of common prosperity and well-being based upon justice."

What future the plan for a GEA holds may well rest upon the degree of security and economic stability achieved in Asia after the war. The Japanese recently have been pleading that the exigencies of war forced them to exact certain requirements from the GEA member nations but that the war had to be won in order to free the whole GEA from western imperialism. They have maintained that in the postwar world, regardless of Japan's victory or defeat, Japanese leadership in the GEA would assure independence, security, and economic stability. Although the peoples of the GEA who have been antagonized by Japanese domination during wartime may reject these promises now, they may turn to Japanese leadership at some future time if something approaching these promises is not forthcoming in the postwar settlement. Life in the GEA under Japanese supervision may seem less grim in retrospect, particularly when viewed in context with the Japanese promise of better things in the postwar world. Whether or not the Japanese are ever able to make another attempt at establishing a GEA, the dream of a Pan-Asia, an "Asia for Asiatics," will undoubtedly hold a potent appeal for the people of Asia.

CHAPTER VI

SUBSEQUENT VIEWS ON THE JAPANESE ECONOMY

During the spring and summer of 1945 much time and effort was expended in assessing the economy of Japan. It was readily acknowledged by persons, like myself, involved in the collection, analysis, dissemination and exploitation of economic intelligence on Japan, that much of this intelligence was "soft," it was based on guesstimates. It was obvious that economic collapse was taking place, though specific data on all aspects of Japanese economy were not available. The Joint Intelligence Staff which produced the Weekly Summary for the Joint Intelligence Committee generally had a conservative view. It was not its practice to make dogmatic statements, hence it was cautious in forecasting the utter collapse of Japan.

After the surrender of Japan, teams from the United States Strategic Bombing Survey (USSBS) went to Japan to assess the effectiveness of the aerial bombing which had taken place. They prepared a report on "The Effects of Strategic Bombing on Japan's War Economy."[17] This included an Appendix A on the U.S. Economic Intelligence on Japan. The persons who prepared this unclassified Report did not seem to have had access to the Weekly Summary of the Joint Intelligence Committee, perhaps because it was classified as SECRET.

The USSBS noted that some of the United States estimates of Japan's wartime economy had been conservative and that Japan's "Productive capacity" had been over-estimated. Further estimates were too conservative in stating that "stock piles and imports were sufficient to support capacity production." These overly generous estimates were used during the early years of the Pacific War and perhaps were conditioned by the intelligence failure on the Japanese entry into the war and on Pearl Harbor. By the spring and summer of 1945, however, such estimates were not being made in the Weekly Summary.

The Report of the USSBS noted that there were "three causes of error in the various estimates of Japanese production: lack of basic data, failure to consider the overall situation in making estimates for individual items, and the omission of administrative, cultural and psychological factors." Actually, this criticism was not valid for the economic intelligence which was included in the Weekly Summary. The Weekly Summary included a number of articles on political and psychological intelligence. The Joint Intelligence Staff took a very broad view of Japan.

During the occupation of Japan many studies were made of different aspects of Japan's economy. Various Reparation Commissions were active in Japan and Japanese-occupied areas. They prepared reports on the Japanese development of its own economy and in the economies of areas it conquered. Little efforts were made, however, to analyze in detail the accuracy of the economic intelligence which had been collected during the Pacific War.

The economic intelligence which was disseminated through the <u>Weekly Summary</u> played a role in the decision-making process of the United States government. In the spring and summer of 1945 the <u>Weekly Summary</u> was read regularly by President Truman and other high officials. The Special Articles and Notes on the deterioration of the Japanese economy, on the Japanese will to resist, on the Japanese exploitation of Southeast Asia and on many other subjects had an influence on these readers.

The United States has continued to carry on economic intelligence activities since World War II, though there is no separate agency for economic intelligence. Today there is a very vast apparatus for gathering intelligence of various kinds through electronic means. The so-called SIGINT Revolution was discussed in a Military History Symposium at the United States Air Force Academy in October of 1988. This openness is quite in contrast with the secretiveness of the days of ULTRA and MAGIC.

Philip Knightley in his 1987 book, aptly titled <u>The Second Oldest Profession</u>, discusses the current status of intelligence.[18] He notes that the CIA spends at least 1.5 billion dollars a year and that the National Security Agency, "the technological side of the American espionage system," probably spends 3.5 billion dollars a year. The rest of the American intelligence community probably spends 2.5 billion dollars a year for a grand total of 7.5 billion dollars a year. The manpower of the American intelligence agencies is conservatively estimated at 150,000 persons, though it should be noted that the Russians use close to an estimated million people in their intelligence networks. Thus, we are faced, in Knightley's words "with an intelligence community which has grown to a size and power which is unprecedented. It is so big and expensive that we can only guess at its size and costs. But there is no doubt about its power." According to Knightley, writing in 1987, "The new thrust (in intelligence) is on the economic front. In a polycentric but economically interdependent world, intelligence about trade, commodity prices, tariffs, financial pacts, currency levels, oil prices, producers' cartels and government attitudes to them, has become as important--more important in many people's views--than military information."

The efforts in economic intelligence during the Pacific War seem very small in contrast with the vast efforts of the present day. Yet the British and American economic intelligence officers, though few in numbers, were able to make useful contributions in estimating the strength of the Japanese. It was in part on the basis of their analyses that strategic and military decisions and actions were taken which weakened Japan's economy and brought about its collapse. This book has been designed to draw attention to and reproduce some of the available economic intelligence on Japan in the spring and summer of 1945 from the Weekly Summary of the Joint Intelligence Committee of the Joint Chiefs of Staff. This economic intelligence needs to be read and studied in the present day. In the words of George Santayana: "Those who cannot remember the past are condemned to repeat it."

APPENDIX

Background Articles on Economic

Activities in Japan and Japanese-Occupied Areas

WEEKLY SUMMARY

> *"—A brief summary highlighting the military, political, economic, and psychological situation. Pronounced trends affecting current operations or pointing toward counter-action are emphasized. Detailed descriptions of military operations, unless conducted under unusual conditions or depicting advance tactics or technique, are avoided."*

Japanese Operation of the Bawdwin Mines in Northern Burma—A Final Analysis

Ever since the Japanese occupation of northern Burma in the spring of 1942, considerable Allied interest has centered in the status of the Bawdwin mines, the largest source of lead and zinc known to have been available to the Japanese during the war. In the prewar years the Bawdwin output was about 74,000 metric tons of lead and 45,000 metric tons of zinc annually. These mines and their accessory installations, all located in and near Namtu, in the Upper Shan States, were subjected to a denial program by the withdrawing British, as previously reported.[1]

Evidence presented about 6 months ago [2] indicated that the Japanese had overcome the denial difficulties to some extent and had restored the mines to partial operation in February 1943. The status of the operation has been followed closely since the last report by the same U. S. Government nonferrous-metals expert who collected the mass of information on which that summary was based. His work was climaxed in March of this year, following the Allied reoccupation of the area, by a personal inspection of the Bawdwin installations and by interviews with some of the personnel associated with the enterprise during Japanese occupation.

The newly available intelligence corroborates the earlier report that the Japanese began actual mining operations in February 1943. It reveals, however, that mining stopped in September 1944 and that the mine was completely closed down in the following November. The on-the-spot investigation showed that the Japanese apparently mined a total of about 140,000 metric tons of ore during their 19 months of operation instead of the 180,000 metric tons previously estimated. The ore output actually achieved in this period was only 21 percent of the "normal" prewar rate rather than the 28 percent estimated earlier. Because the richer lower levels were flooded,

[1] See "The Bawdwin Mines—A Japanese State in Burma," *Weekly Summary*, Number 15 (21 April 1943), pp. 16–19.

[2] See "Japanese Operation of the Bawdwin Mines in Northern Burma, *Weekly Summary*, Number 99 (30 November 1944), pp. 29–30.

Japanese production was confined to ore from the six more nearly exhausted upper levels with lesser metal values.

Apparently about 132,000 metric tons of this ore were milled. The lead content of the mill products was equivalent to about 14,000 metric tons, and the zinc content to about 8,000 metric tons. It was reliably reported to the inspector that the Japanese did not ship any of the mill products which they themselves made during their operations, and this statement is provisionally accepted.

However, the Japanese shipped out, from stocks abandoned by the British, virtually all of the 30,000 metric tons of lead; some 2,000 metric tons each of copper matte, nickel-cobalt speiss, and coarse and float concentrates; 4,000 metric tons of zinc concentrates; 3,200 metric tons of coke; and 400 metric tons of miscellaneous materials, including hard lead. Another 1,000 metric tons of refined lead were produced in the refinery at Namtu from stocked pig lead, and this also was shipped. Rather surprisingly, the Japanese shipped out apparently only a minor part of the 98,000 metric tons of zinc concentrates left in storage dams at Bawdwin by the British.

Japanese operation of the refinery was limited to 3 months in the autumn of 1944. As indicated in the previous report, the Japanese did not operate the smelter during their tenure. The concentrating mill was not run continuously, and at least 25,000 to 30,000 metric tons of ore mined by the Japanese were left lying on the ground untreated.

The British denial program consisted of damaging essential equipment and dispersing trained personnel. Aside from dynamiting some machinery in the concentrator and smelter, the British paid particular attention to rendering power facilities and electrical equipment inoperative. Orders for damage, however, were not altogether effectively carried out.

By February 1943 the Japanese had succeeded in restoring the auxiliary Konnyaung hydroelectric power plant to operation, thus obtaining power for partial operation of the mine, the concentrator, and the necessary auxiliary equipment which also had been restored as required. About 60 to 70 percent of the dispersed skilled personnel had been gathered up by mid-1942, and these workers, reinforced by unskilled workmen, carried out the repairs and subsequent operation under Japanese supervisors.

The ore output under Japanese operation increased from 100 metric tons a day in February 1943 to 400 metric tons a day in January

1944. The destruction of the Konnyaung power plant by bombing during that month cut production to 10 to 12 tons a day until April 1944, when the Japanese succeeded in restoring the Mansam Falls power plant to partial operation. Production then quickly increased to 400 metric tons a day and remained at this level until mining stopped in September 1944.

The Japanese decision to discontinue operation at Bawdwin apparently was made in August 1944, and shipments of equipment and supplies from Japan were stopped at that time. It may be surmised that interruption of transport both within Burma and in the sea lanes was the determining factor, as operation at Bawdwin at that time was proceeding at the maximum rate achieved under Japanese control.

The Japanese were forced to import equipment and supplies to restore the mines to the degree of operating condition achieved, but the net effect of their tenure was serious damage to the property. They injured the mine itself by inefficient, destructive, and wasteful operation, and damaged, removed, and destroyed equipment when they withdrew. However, Allied bombing prevented the Japanese from running some of the machinery over a spur line into the river as planned at the time of their withdrawal. The damage caused by earlier Allied air attacks on the Konnyaung power plant, on concentration and flotation mills, and on machine shops was another consequence of Japanese control.

The U. S. Government nonferrous-metals expert who visited the area estimates that 35 to 45 percent of the installations have been severely damaged. He conjectures that with suitably high priorities, and with satisfactory personnel and supervision, the mines may be restored to 60 to 95 percent working order (depending upon the condition of the parts still flooded) in about 9 months, the smelter and refinery in 1 to 2 months, power facilities in about 6 months, the transportation system in about 2 or 3 months, and the various auxiliary installations in 5 to 6 months. The concentrating mill has been 95 percent demolished and may require 9 months to a year to rebuild and equip. The mines, mill, and smelter might be put into effective operating condition in 12 to 15 months after renovation begins.

The Development of Aluminous Shales in Northern China

In the last few months numerous sources have mentioned the development of a "light metals" industry in northern China, consisting of the mining and treatment of aluminous shale deposits useful as sources of alumina and hence aluminum.

Because the success of the U. S. offensive in the Southwest Pacific has almost cut off Japanese imports of high-grade bauxite, Japan's position with regard to this basic material for aluminum production has grown much worse within the last few months. Aluminous ores other than bauxite are available in Manchuria and Korea, but these materials cannot be processed in the standard Bayer plants designed to produce alumina from bauxite without considerable plant conversion.

It is estimated, however, that non-Bayer and converted Bayer plants in Japan, Korea, and Manchuria now have the capacity to produce annually over 300,000 metric tons of alumina. Direct military requirements for alumina at peak 1944 rates, without regard for bomb damage to the aircraft industry, were estimated at 388,000 metric tons a year. It may be assumed that the newly reported development in northern China was intended to make up part of the balance.

Large deposits of aluminous shales are known to exist in northern China, especially in the coal-producing areas. Information from ground sources and interpretations of aerial photographs indicate that deposits are being worked in at least two widely separated localities: namely, the Poshan coal mining district of central Shantung and the Kailan coal-mining area of northern Hopeh. Processing equipment is being installed in central Shantung.

The aerial photographs show that the mining operations in both areas consist largely of numerous scattered surface diggings which could readily be operated with a minimum of skilled labor and mechanized equipment. Ground reports indicate that the total output of aluminous raw materials from these localities may be about 60,000 metric tons a month. If all of this material were used for alumina production, it could represent an alumina output of about 240,000 metric tons annually. Assuming that none is intended for production of refractories, it would appear that northern China could produce over 60 percent of Japanese requirements as of 1944 for aluminous raw materials for the production of aluminum.

From available information on shipments from this area, it is assumed that the material mined has been sent to Japan, Manchuria, and Korea for processing. However, aerial photographs show that a large plant is under construction about 2½ miles south of Changtien, near the village of Nanting, and very close to the most extensive aluminous shale-mining operations seen in Shantung. Examination of photographs of the installation indicates that it is intended to produce alumina from the local aluminous shale by a kiln process. So far as can now be determined, no installation for the electrolytic production of metallic aluminum has been erected. The capacity of the new plant cannot yet be estimated, but it is obviously an undertaking of significant size.

The Location of Japan's Industrial War-making Capacity

An estimate of the industrial war-making potential of a country involves consideration of a large variety of diversified factors, all of them mutually interdependent. Thus factories producing guns depend upon plants making machine tools and both depend upon the supply of steel, copper, and other metals. Because the relative potential of these different links in the industrial chain in Japan varies greatly, the total war-making potential cannot be adequately reduced to a common denominator for the purpose of arriving at a single percentage.

Considering only industries such as arsenals, munitions plants, aircraft factories, and the like, which produce end products of military importance, it is estimated that from 80 to 90 percent of Japan's industrial war-making potential is located in the main Japanese islands. These end-product industries, however, do not truly reflect the practical limits of Japan's war-making potential in the home islands. Particularly in the basic manufacturing industries, it will be found that a considerable discrepancy exists between the available capacity and the actual output, which is conditioned by limitations on the quantities of raw materials that can be transported and by other factors.

Armament and Munitions for Ground Forces

Approximately 80 percent of the present Japanese output of armament and munitions for ground forces is concentrated in the main Japanese islands, for the most part in Honshu and Kyushu. Out of 48 major arsenals, private arsenals, and combat-vehicle plants now producing or capable of producing equipment for the Japanese ground forces, only 3 are located on the Asiatic Mainland—at Mukden, Manchuria, and at Heijo and Jinsen, Korea. The Mukden Arsenal is the only plant on the Asiatic Mainland capable of producing heavy guns and tanks. A number of former Chinese arsenals in northern and central China have been put to use by the Japanese, but these plants produce only small arms and a negligible amount of cannon, and their aggregate output is of minor proportions.

Iron and Steel

Only about 45 percent of the total Japanese output of pig iron is being produced in the home islands, and of this quantity only about 30 percent is derived from domestic ores. The bulk of the pig iron which is being produced on the Asiatic Mainland is shipped to Japan for processing, and approximately 65 percent of steel ingots and 84 percent of rolled steel are being produced in the main islands.

Aircraft

Over 90 percent of all types of Japanese combat aircraft is produced in the home islands. Manufacturing facilities for Japanese aircraft on the Asiatic Mainland are small and are now devoted almost entirely to the production of low-performance training planes.

Shipping and Shipbuilding

Virtually all the shipbuilding capacity of the Japanese Empire is in the home islands, and only a few small yards, mostly for building wooden ships, are located in Manchuria and Korea. Also, fairly extensive shipbuilding capacity exists along the China coast, but the aggregate tonnage produced in such yards has been and probably will continue to be of minor proportions.

Oil

About 50 percent of the oil production and over 90 percent of the refining capacity of the inner zone are in Japan proper.

Aluminum

About 60 percent of the Japanese production of aluminum is concentrated in the main islands, but of this quantity probably less than 10 percent is derived from ores located in Japan proper.

Coal

Japanese industry in the home islands draws heavily upon the Asiatic Mainland for supplies of coal and must rely upon the mainland for a substantial percentage of its total furnace coke requirements.

Copper and Other Nonferrous Metals

The loss of the southern areas will deprive Japan of her main source of various nonferrous metals. The preponderant part of existing stockpiles and the potential production of nonferrous metals within the inner zone (with the exception of alumina) is located in the main Japanese islands.

Railroad Equipment

It is believed that at least 77 percent of Japan's total capacity for producing locomotives is located in Japan proper. The corresponding figure for railroad cars and other railroad equipment is probably not less than 74 percent.

Intentions and Capabilities of the Japanese for Transferring Their Industrial War-making Potential to the Asiatic Mainland

There have been repeated reports of Japanese plans for the transfer of industries to the Asiatic mainland, and available evidence indicates a trend in this direction. Japanese broadcasts have stated at various times that production of arms and aircraft in Manchuria and Korea will be increased and have even suggested that plants manufacturing aircraft and other war goods will be moved from Japan as an air-defense measure. In addition, the Japanese Government has announced the definite determination to strengthen the war potential of of Manchuria, Korea, and northern China, pledging material and financial assistance, in order to provide a greater degree of self-sufficiency for the Japanese armed forces in these territories.

Evidence is quite conclusive that thus far the actual transfer of Japanese industries to the Asiatic mainland has not proceeded very far and has been of relatively minor proportions. There is no evidence to date which indicates that major war plants have been involved in any transfer made or contemplated. Until now the movement has involved only the shipment of idle mining and basic industrial and chemical equipment in order to increase the production of essential raw materials to make up for the loss of supplies from Southern areas, and to alleviate transportation difficulties by processing raw materials on the spot, thereby reducing the bulk of materials to be transported to the home islands. It is believed that this trend will continue substantially unchanged and that parallel with this program efforts will be made to expand the production of munitions, as well as aircraft and parts, on the Asiatic mainland. It is also believed, however, that this expansion will not be undertaken at the expense of capacity and production in the home islands and that it will be limited by the availability of surplus machinery and tools on the mainland and in Japan.

With the loss of oil from the East Indies, much emphasis has been given to the expansion of synthetic oil and substitute fuel production in the inner zone, especially in Manchuria and northern China. Since fuel is an item of high priority, it is reasonable to assume that the greatest effort will be exerted in this direction. Again, however, there is no indication that any existing synthetic oil plants in Japan are being shifted to the Asiatic mainland, nor is it believed that an attempt of this nature will be made in the future.

Rate of Movement Involved

The rate of movement of processing capacity from Japan to the Asiatic mainland cannot be gauged with accuracy, but it now seems reasonably clear that the movement which has been consummated during the last year has been of slight proportions. There is some reason to expect that the Japanese are now attempting to accelerate the transfer of industrial capacity, but as yet it is impossible to determine the current rate of movement, which, as stated above, remains relatively low.

Capabilities

Factors limiting the ability of the Japanese to move industry to the Asiatic mainland include very complex engineering and transport problems, the difficulties of organization and administration, the availability of machine tools, and the necessity for transferring or training personnel. These limiting factors will be aggravated further by increasing Allied interference.

Even should the Japanese immediately decide to move or accelerate the movement of war industries to the Asiatic mainland, it is not believed that the capacity for the manufacture of military equipment on the mainland could be increased by as much as 50 percent in a year's time. The present capacity of arsenals and munition plants on the mainland may be nearly adequate to meet for some time to come the defensive requirements of present Japanese forces in small arms, mortars, light machine guns, hand grenades, and small-caliber ammunition. However, the production of heavier artillery weapons and ammunition on the mainland, as well as that of tanks and other automotive equipment, is very inadequate. No manufacturers of signal and precision equipment are known to operate on the mainland,

and the present capacity there for the production of aircraft, shipping, and some other essential war needs is relatively of negligible consequence.

As for the requirements of present Japanese forces in China and Manchuria for active defensive operations, it is estimated that 2 or 3 years would be required to transfer to Asia sufficient potential to meet them completely. Allied reconnaissance has revealed very extensive ordnance and munitions storage areas in Manchuria and Korea, and the quantities of existing stocks on hand, about which so little is definitely known, will have a great bearing on the length of time during which local forces could be adequately supplied under active defensive requirements. Nevertheless it is believed that Japan would require on the Continent an industrial base several times larger than the one now existing there in order to meet active defensive requirements over an extended period.

The Importance and Vulnerability of Japanese Lines of Communication

To an unusual degree Japan's lines of water and land communication provide indispensable support to her sustained war production and her deployment of armed forces and matériel. In large measure Japan's war industries are not located in close proximity to their necessary sources of supply.[1] Japan proper is currently dependent upon imports to maintain about 70 percent of steel production and 95 percent of aluminum production; also imported are 55 percent of salt and 10 percent of essential food. Basic industries in many cases are almost entirely dependent upon remote stocks of coal, coke, pig iron, and other raw or semi-processed materials. End-product industries are likewise in many cases dependent upon receiving a regular flow of semi-processed materials and component parts from other areas. Subcontracting is believed to be quite extensive not only within local areas but also between widely separated areas. It is believed that local stocks for some important industries are very much limited and that the Japanese will not be able to make such industries self-sufficient or independent of the regular and sustained flow of traffic. Significant war production, however, could be continued for a limited period following virtually complete severance of communications. Obviously, the industries having greatest significance in the Japanese war effort would continue to receive the highest priority as regards both imports and the internal moving of supplies. Thus a partial interdiction of any line of communication does not necessarily indicate that the industry depending upon such supply route would necessarily suffer loss of production.

Railroad System

With the progressive deterioration of the Japanese shipping situation, a greater burden is being thrown upon the highly organized but

[1] See "The Location of Japan's Industrial War-making Capacity," *Weekly Summary*, Number 122 (10 May 1945), pp. 15–17.

relatively limited railroad system under Japanese control. The main rail line from northern China across southern Manchuria and down through Korea carries a very substantial part of the pig iron, coal, and other essential materials imported by Japan proper from these areas. Rail traffic in Japan proper (see the map inside the back cover) is likewise of the highest importance to the main industrial areas as regards the transport of raw, semi-finished, and finished products between the various war centers. Although coastwise and Inland Sea shipping normally carried more tonnage than the railroads, the latter now have become far more important than formerly as a result of shipping difficulties. In an emergency the railroad system in Japan proper would be essential to the rapid deployment of Japan's defense forces.

There are about 17,500 miles of rail lines in Japan proper, of which mileage about 50 percent is located south and west of Tokyo. The rugged interior makes railroad construction difficult on all the islands, and only a few routes are of major importance. The Japanese railroad system is much more susceptible to air attack than were any of the European systems, owing to its comparatively small size, its predominantly single track routes, the scarcity of alternative routes and rail centers, and the abundance of major engineering structures. In most cases recuperability is high, and to dislocate seriously Japan's economy for an appreciable period of time an intensive program of sustained attack would be required. Prior to invasion or for any temporary period it should be possible to interdict rail traffic almost completely and isolate main industrial or strategic areas.

Road System

Japan's road system is relatively unimportant except for local movements. For the most part, roads are poor and not vulnerable to air attacks.

Inland Water and Sea Communications

The very great importance to Japan of ocean shipping is well known. With all communications to the southern areas effectively interdicted, the importance of future sea communications will be limited primarily to the maintenance of shipping routes in the Yellow Sea and across the

Straits of Tsushima and the Sea of Japan. These routes will continue to be of the greatest importance to Japan in maintaining her war economy, and eventually in the support of her military forces in the final defense of Japan proper, Korea, Manchuria, and northern China.

A substantial proportion of the internal trade of Japan moves by way of coastal and inland waterways. The Inland Sea is the most important of Japan's waterways and contains the greatest concentration of shipping in the Japanese Empire.

The general vulnerability of Japan's shipping to Allied air and submarine attacks needs no elaboration. The tremendous concentrations of shipping in the Shimonoseki–Wakamatsu and Osaka–Kobe areas of the Inland Sea region should prove particularly vulnerable to air attacks. Mining operations and attacks on port facilities and ferry terminals will add greatly to Japan's shipping difficulties. It must be borne in mind, however, that minimum necessary communications cannot be interdicted immediately by ship sinkings and that it is difficult to neutralize small boats operating at night with improvised landing facilities.

The Importance of the Port of Fusan

Fusan in southeastern Korea is the gateway to the Asiatic Continent from the Islands of Japan. Ferry distance from Shimonoseki is only 121 miles. This route long has been the funnel through which much of the passenger and high priority traffic has traveled from the Asiatic mainland to Japan. With the decrease in available merchant shipping, the Japanese have endeavored to utilize the "overland route" which has its terminus at Fusan.

This shift to land transportation occasioned certain administrative difficulties. The Japanese established the Chosen Kairiku Unyu K. K. (Land and Sea Transportation Company) to control and coordinate land and sea transportation in Korea. A Continental Transportation Council was also organized to undertake the smooth interchange of essential materials between Japan and other parts of the mainland. The Shipping Management Association offices, located at Korean and Japanese ports, determine the routes for particular commodities. A general trend has been to use Fusan for shipping of essential war materials and passengers and for movement of troops and military supplies. Other Korean ports, especially in the northeast, are used for the movement of heavy raw materials.

Fusan is well equipped with rail facilities. It is the terminus of the double-track Shingishu-Fusan rail line, which connects Korea and Manchuria. A parallel rail line in interior Korea also terminates at Fusan. The freight car ferries between Fusan and Shimonoseki and between Fusan and Hakata have been prepared for the direct movement to war factories in northern Kyushu of materials from North China and Manchuria, eliminating the necessity of transshipment.

The harbor facilities are excellent. Two new piers have been constructed, doubling the capacity of the port. The four piers range in length from 1,300 to 1,950 feet.

The Japanese have built alternate ports in southern Korea to use in emergencies or to carry specialized cargoes. Masan to the west is an older port which has recently been expanded. Near it is the naval port of Chinkai. Farther west, the port of Reisui, connected by rail with southwestern and central Korea, has had a considerable increase in freight traffic. Both Masan and Reisui have ferry services with Shimonoseki and ports in Kyushu. To the east of Fusan are the ports of Urusan and Hoko, which can be used as alternates and are now being used for fishing boats and movement of some commodities. In addition, there are other small ports which do not have rail connections. Ports on the southwest of Korea—Mokpo, Gunsan, and Jinsen—could be used but have limited loading and shipping capacities and would involve longer marine routes.

The northeastern Korean ports of Yuki, Rashin, and Seishin are being extensively used for shipments of heavy goods from Manchuria and North China. They involve a longer marine route but are within the protected Sea of Japan. The distance between Seishin and Tsuruga is 457 miles and that between Seishin and Shimonoseki is 522 miles. Other ports along the east coast of Korea—Joshin, Konan, and Gensan—are now used for movements of goods produced in their immediate hinterland but could be utilized for the continental trade if necessary.

Despite these alternate routes, Fusan is the vital center for trade and shipping between the mainland and Japan. If Fusan were denied to the Japanese, extensive reorganization of the transportation system would be necessary. The alternate ports could be of use for short periods of time but would not be able to take the place of Fusan.

Japan's Inner Mongolian Industrial Base

Japan has long had plans in Inner Mongolia, the puppet state of which she calls Mengchiang, for developing an industrial base that could provide support to the continental war machine, particularly in basic industries. Mengchiang has coal, mostly noncoking, and iron in abundance and some mica, asbestos, salt, and kaolin, as well as a surplus of wool. In the early days of occupation attention was focused on the exploitation of coal, iron ore, and wool for shipment to Japan. The inland position of this area, now an important asset to the war economy of the mainland, was a distinct handicap in the long and difficult overland haul for shipment to the home islands.

Loss of the rich iron ore from Malaya and the Philippines has increased the relative importance of Mengchiang to Japan, and also to Manchuria, where there has been a chronic insufficiency of ore of high iron content. An intensified program of development was instituted in 1942 with the financial and technical aid of the Manchuria Industrial Development Corporation.

Mengchiang is still insufficiently served by railway facilities, but two industrial centers have developed under the Japanese plans—one at Hsuanhua, near the Lungyen iron mines, and one at Tatung near very large and rich coal deposits and also near new iron-ore workings. Kalgan, the old commercial center between northern China and Mongolia, is now the political and financial nerve center of Japan's Inner Mongolian base.

At Hsuanhua two iron works are reported, one with 50 small blast furnaces and the other with 5. The total yearly capacity of the two plants is estimated at 183,000 metric tons. A steel mill also is reported in this area and a small-arms arsenal.

In the Tatung area, expansion of coal mining has been accompanied by the reported construction of a coal liquefaction plant at Kouchuan, and an iron works has been seen from the air. The Tatung area also has an alcohol plant and a calcium-carbide factory. The scale of operations in both centers is small, and progress has been impeded by many difficulties. The export of coal from Tatung to the coast has been severely limited in recent months by the use of available rail capacity for shipping out iron ore from Lungyen and pig iron from Hsuanhua.

The nonmineral resources of Mengchiang are limited, and the population is sparse. There are vast areas of desert and grazing land, with little intensive farming. The industrial development, therefore, has no significant body of labor to draw upon and no natural advantage except the rich deposits of iron and coal. The long overland haul to other centers is still a handicap and is a major reason for the attempt to process the raw materials in the area.

As mining and smelting plants are the principal industries of Mengchiang, this area now has little strategic economic value except as it is linked to the end-product industries of Manchuria and Japan. There is small likelihood that a fully integrated industrial economy that could support a continental army will arise quickly in this region. The combined agricultural resources of Mengchiang and northern China are sufficient to provide food and clothing for Japanese and puppet troops now garrisoned in the two areas. It is believed, however, that production of small arms and ammunition in both areas is barely sufficient to supply garrisoned troops for antiguerrilla operations.

The Economic Importance of Korea to Japan

The economic importance of Korea to Japan has been as a land bridge to the Continent and as a source of supply for foods and metals. Only in recent years and under the impetus of the demands of war has Korea's industrial development been a major consideration to the Japanese. The principal impetus to industrialization in this highly agricultural economy has been the wealth of recently developed hydroelectric power. The natural resources of the area are modest and are not particularly favorable to the development of modern industry under international competition. The large deposits of iron ore are low in iron content; the rich deposits are small. There are substantial quantities of coal, but it is anthracite or lignite and thus not the best coal for industrial purposes. The Japanese have developed deposits of alunite and alum shale as a substitute for bauxite for the alumina industry, but there is some evidence that the processes employed were not successful and that the effort has been abandoned in favor of the better grade alum shales of northern China. Excellent deposits of magnesite have been reported in Korea, and there are small quantities of copper, lead, and zinc. Gold and silver and numerous other metals and minerals are found in modest amounts. Korea is relatively rich in forest products and has a large production of textile fibers and foods that serve as a base for industry. In general, except for the hydroelectric power, Korea has no great natural advantage for the development of heavy industry. Many of the plants now operating have been fostered either by the Japanese Government or by large Japanese interests and have been oriented to the supply of the Japanese economy and not in terms of Korea's needs. Without such backing many of the present establishments would be handicapped. It may prove cheaper in some cases for Korea after the war to import products from abroad than to maintain the industry.

Korea's hydroelectric power has been developed almost entirely since 1936 and has made possible the rapid expansion of industry in the war years. The larger plants are located in the north and east on the Yalu River and its tributaries the Choshin, Fusen, and Kyosen Rivers.

These plants supply the most important industrial areas in Korea, particularly those centered at Seishin, Kanko Keijo, Heijo, and Shingishu.

Heavy industry is essentially a wartime development in Korea. The Kenjiho Iron Works (near Heijo) which are based partly on local rich ores, date from 1918, and further expansion began after 1936. Japan's war program made possible the development of other iron and steel works using lean ores mined in Korea and made usable by concentration. Most of these plants are of small scale except the works at Seishin established about 1940. Korea's steel ingot capacity is integrated with the iron works and is estimated at 600,000 metric tons a year, but rolling mill capacity is less than one-third of this amount. The chief center for rolling mills is at Kenjiho. There is thought to be no rolling mill capacity at Seishin, and the only other rolling mill development is a small plant at Joshin (on the canal between Seishin and Kanko). Fabrication is centered at Heijo and Keijo.

The light metal industry is another development born of Japan's war needs. Alumina and aluminum plants have been established in Korea as an integral part of Japan's program for self-supply within areas close to the home islands. Raw materials are obtained principally from China. The aluminum plants are located at Yoshi (near Shingishu), Konan (near Kanko), Genzan, and Chinnampo (near Heijo), where an abundance of hydroelectric power is easily available. The consuming industries are the aircraft plants in Japan and those newly established in Korea.

Based also on the available hydroelectric power, a very considerable chemical industry has developed. One of the largest chemical works in the Japanese Empire is at Konan, near the hydroelectric plants on the Fusen and Choshin Rivers. These works produce sulphuric acid, nitrogen, calcium carbide, magnesium, bromine, caustic soda, and soda ash. Other chemical plants at Konan produce glycerol and explosives. As another part of the program of self-supply from the inner areas, a synthetic fuel industry has developed at the lignite mines in Agochi, Eian, and Sanchoku along the eastern coast. Another wartime development is a large-scale alcohol plant using wood waste from the saw mills at Shingishu.

As Japan's primary interest in Korea has been for the supply of raw materials and food, the development of an integrated economy has been of very recent date. This development has taken place chiefly in the Heijo and Keijo areas, which are commercial centers of very ancient origin. Easy transportation has brought the products from the surrounding agricultural and mining areas and from abroad to build these two largest cities of Korea. A nucleus for the development of a machine industry had existed in these cities before the war in the railway shops and the workshops that were making mining machinery and agricultural equipment. With the progress of Japan's war plans, the arsenal at Heijo was expanded, and at both Heijo and Keijo aircraft plants and plants for the manufacture of machinery and machine parts have been established and expanded into the surrounding areas.

Industries of consumer goods have been slow to develop in Korea, although the character of the economy, with a large labor supply and home market and the less favorable conditions for heavy industry, favored a first development of light industry. The Korean market for factory-made consumer goods has been supplied primarily from Japan, but a high proportion of Korea's consumer goods is still made in handicraft workshops. The modern cotton textile industry has developed mostly since 1933. The earliest mill began operation in 1922, but most of the others are of much later date. The synthetic fiber mills are a recent development. The silk filatures are an earlier development organized not in relation to the Korean domestic economy but essentially for her export trade. Other consumer goods are produced on a very small scale, and there has been a very heavy dependence on imports from Japan. The few large-scale food-processing establishments includes some wheat flour mills, a sugar refinery, and breweries for *sake* and beer. A mill for corn products, which originally made sizing for the cotton mills, is now reported to be making alcohol.

In a very general way Korea's industrial pattern has located the machinery and metal industries in the West and Central Districts; the chemicals in the North and East; and the textiles in the South and Central. The recent developments, however, have brought about a fuller integration of industries in the greater industrial areas than was formerly evident. The greater industrial areas are comprised of groups of cities which make up an integrated complex. In the northwest the industrial area reaches from Shingishu through Heijo to Kaishu (on the coast between Heijo and Keijo) and includes both heavy and light industry and final machine-processing. A second major industrial complex is located in the area from Keijo to Jinsen (the port of Keijo) but is more particularly engaged in final processing. The third complex includes Seishin, Joshin, and Konan along the northeastern coast and has iron and steel works and rolling mills, aluminum works, heavy chemicals, and, at Konan, a large machine works that is believed to be available for the supply of the whole complex.

Most of the large-scale industry of Korea is in Japanese hands. The large metal works, chemical plants, machine shops, and aircraft plants are all either directly controlled from Japan or are subsidiaries of Japanese corporations. Very little Korean capital has taken part in the development of modern industry and almost none in the war industries.

Korean railways have been developed primarily to supply Japan and to hurdle through traffic to the Continent. More recently they have been integrated into a network for the supply of the expanding Korean industry. Because of their strategic importance, they have been planned not only to supplement the carrying capacity of one another but to act as alternate lines in case of trouble. The main trunk line is double-tracked practically throughout and runs from Fusan, the port nearest Japan, to Shingishu on the Manchurian border and passes through Korea's two greatest commercial centers, Heijo and Keijo. The system of next importance to the Japanese connects Seishin and Rashin (northeast of Seishin) with Manchuria.

The sea ports of greatest importance in Korea at present are Rashin, on the northeastern coast, and Fusan, at the southern tip of the peninsula. Prior to the war the western coast ports of Jinsen and Chinnampo were of major importance to Korean economy, but the emphasis during the war has shifted from the western coast to the southern and eastern coasts, from which sea routes to Japan are both safer and more direct. On the northeastern coast the ports of Seishin, Rashin, Yuki, Konan, and Genzan have been developed to provide additional means of export for the continental goods bound for Japan. On the southern coast the facilities at Fusan are supplemented by the ports of Masan, Reisui, and Moppo. There are numerous smaller ports along the eastern coast of Korea which appear also to be active, but Rashin, with its alternates, and Fusan, with its alternates, are the ports of principal importance.

The Economic Importance of Kyushu

Kyushu's primary importance to Japan's war economy is in the coal resources of the northwestern part of the island: the Chikuho coal field east of Fukuoka, the Miike field near Omuta, and other fields at Sasebo and Karatsu. These four fields produce about half of Japan's coal. Much of this coal is exported to Honshu by rail through the Moji–Shimonoseki tunnels or by barge through the Inland Sea.

Based upon the local resources of coal, a large concentration of heavy industry has been developed in Kyushu. Rather than being centered in one city as is common elsewhere in Japan, these industries have grown up in a string of cities running from Moji through Yawata to Fukuoka along the northern shore, with subsidiary areas in Karatsu, Sasebo, Nagasaki, and Omuta. In these cities imported raw materials can most easily be combined with coal from the near-by collieries, and the finished products can be shipped by water or by the rail line along the coast. The large iron and steel industry is dependent upon imported ore and upon some imported coking coal needed to mix with the local coal supplies. A nonferrous smelting industry, using imported zinc, lead, and copper ores and concentrates and imported aluminous shale, and the processing of bauxite are located here because of the proximity of the coal fields and the electric power thereby developed. Heavy chemicals and synthetic fuel industries also utilize the coal resources.

The products from the heavy industry centers in Kyushu have in the past been exported in large part to the more highly developed industrial centers on Honshu. With the present difficulties of transportation and the desire for regional self-sufficiency, more of these products are going into local aircraft, shipbuilding, machine-tool, and ordnance industries, although the industries of the northwestern Kyushu area as a whole are not too well integrated. Outside northwestern Kyushu there are smaller industrial centers in Nobeoka, Kagoshima, and Yatsushiro, but these areas are dependent upon imported materials for their war industries.

Kyushu has a population of 10 million people, including a substantial number of skilled workers trained in the metallurgical and machine industries. The bulk of the population, however, is engaged in agriculture and fishing. Although rice is not so prominent a crop on the island as in other parts of Japan, the area is self-sufficient in food because of its production of wheat, barley, and vegetables which can be double-cropped with rice in the mild winters.

Because of the mountainous center of Kyushu, the main rail line follows the coast line completely around the island, with short spurs extending inland and in a few places cutting across peninsulas. There is a complex network of rail lines running out from the coal fields to the industrial centers. Most of the transportation of heavy goods away from the island has been handled in the past by coastal shipping utilizing the numerous harbors in the indented coast line. With the recent completion of the Moji–Shimonoseki tunnels, through rail transportation of these products is being effected.

The Economic Importance of Karafuto to Japan

Karafuto, the southern half of Sakhalin Island, has not been of major economic importance to Japan. Because of the cold winters (5 months average below freezing) and the short, cool, rainy summers, Karafuto's climate does not appeal to the Japanese and has not attracted settlers from the home islands.

About 80 percent of Karafuto is forested, principally with stands of coniferous trees of the species Abies and Picea, although at lower altitudes and in the low coastwise districts extensive stands of silver birch, willow, and other trees are found. Those forests were state-owned, and their exploitation provided a considerable part of the governmental revenue. In 1938 felling operations produced 4,752,000 cubic meters of timber, as well as smaller wood for faggots and charcoal. Associated with forestry is the manufacture of wood pulp and paper, the principal industrial products of the island, and in the same year 264,000 metric tons of rayon pulp, some of the best in Japan, and 180,000 metric tons of paper were produced. The Oji Paper Company has a virtual monopoly of the industry in Karafuto, and has factories at Toyohara, Otomari, Ochiai, Maoka, Noda, and Tomarioru in the south, and at Shiratori and Esutoru farther north. At one time Karafuto provided 98 percent of Japan's domestic supply of rayon pulp, but between 1936 and 1941 this figure dropped to less than 50 percent, as Japan expanded the use of local timber in the main islands.

On Karafuto there are rich deposits of bituminous coal, some of which is of coking quality, and lignite, the most important mines being at Kawakami, northwest of Toyohara, and at Ohira, northeast of Esutoru in the north. The other important mining centers are just west of Shikuka at Shiratori, Kashiho, Shiraura, and Naibuchi on the eastern coast and at Naihoro and the Tomarioru district in the west. The total output of coal was stepped up from 645,000 metric tons in 1930 to 3,500,000 metric tons in 1938. It may have been increased to about 4 million metric tons in 1944. Although prospecting and drilling for petroleum has been carried on for a number of years in the southwestern part of the island in the Honto area, there is no evidence of the production of natural petroleum. There are, however, two plants for the production of synthetic oil by low-temperature carbonization at Naihoro in the southwest and at Naibuchi in the southeast, using local coal.

Fishing is the oldest industry in Karafuto, employing 4 percent of the population. The catch consists of herring, salmon, trout, cod, whales, and crab. The bulk of fish for food is principally dried, salted, or canned at centers such as Maoka, Shikuka, and Tomarioru. The greater part of the catch, however, mainly herring, has been used for fertilizer. The 1939 catch, including shellfish and seaweeds, is estimated at 300,000 metric tons.

Only 10 percent of Karafuto's population of 400,000 in 1940 was engaged in agriculture. About 3 percent of the area is arable land, only one-tenth of which was under cultivation in 1938. More land could be used, therefore, for the growth of such crops as oats, rye, peas, beans, and potatoes. Fodder is grown for livestock. As in Hokkaido, there are a number of fair-sized dairy farms. Breeding of deer and fur-bearing animals, especially silver fox, is prominent in some parts.

A railway follows the east coast from Shikuka to Toyohara and the port of Otomari in the south, and by a branch line from Toyohara connects with a shorter line on the west coast running from Honto to Kushunnai. In addition, a number of narrow-gauge tracks, sometimes with horse-drawn cars, haul coal and lumber short distances, feeding into the main lines. Roads parallel the main coast railways, and the road on the eastern coast is continuous to the northern frontier, while cross-country routes connect Shikuka with Esutoru, and Manui with Kushunnai, and lead from Toyohara to Maoka and Honto on the western coast, and south to Otomari and the shores of Aniwa Bay. Sea routes provide connection with Wakkanai on Hokkaido by a ferry service run by the railway company from Otomari, and a coastal service calls at most ports of any size, particularly those in the west, which are more important as shipping points for coal and timber.

The Economic Importance of Hokkaido

Hokkaido has only in the last 75 years become a real part of the Japanese Empire, and even today it is relatively much less important to the Japanese economy than are the other home islands. As the Japanese spread from the Inland Sea region of southern Japan to the north, they found the climate less and less inviting. The severely cold winters and cool summers in Hokkaido discouraged the Japanese colonists. However, as the Russians advanced into eastern Asia, the Japanese felt that it was necessary for them to use Hokkaido as a region for frontier settlement. Into this pioneer zone the Japanese in some cases displaced the small numbers of Ainu tribesmen, who had been carrying on very meager existence. The growth of population in Hokkaido reveals the recency of its settlement. The population in 1870 was 66,000 and had been relatively stable for the previous two or three centuries. However, owing especially to the Japanese policy of military settlements, the population increased to 223,290 in 1880; to 427,128 in 1890; and to 985,304 in 1900. The population in the following decades reached 1,482,400 in 1910; 2,359,183 in 1920; 2,812,335 in 1930; and 3,272,718 in 1940.

Settlement of Hokkaido is mainly along the coasts and in the western plains, for Japanese attempts to encourage settlement of the interior have not met with much success. Thirty percent of the population live in the largest towns, four of which were over the 100,000 mark in 1940: namely, Sapporo, 206,000; Hakodate, 203,000; Otaru, 164,000; and Muroran, 108,000. Only about 11 percent of the land is under cultivation; climate, configuration, and, in some of the eastern lowlands, poor drainage has restricted crop production in some parts. Farms on the whole are larger than in the rest of Japan, and agricultural methods are less intensive, if more up-to-date and involving greater use of draft animals and equipment. In spite of these difficulties, Hokkaido produces a surplus of beans, potatoes, vegetables, and dairy products. Rice, of which barely sufficient is grown to meet the island's needs, is found only in the western and southwestern plains and in the Asahigawa basin. Oats are grown on higher ground in the same areas, and barley and buckwheat are more common in the eastern areas. Vegetables, soy and other beans, and potatoes are produced in large quantities and help to supply deficiency areas in Honshu. A large portion of Japan's white potatoes are grown in Hokkaido. The southern and eastern districts are more suitable for livestock, and sugar beets are important in the Obihiro area.

The coastal regions of Hokkaido, which were the first to be settled by the Japanese, have supported an important fishing industry, particularly along the western and southern shores. Herring and sardine made up most of the catch, which also included salmon, mackerel, and cod. Hokodate, Otaru, Muroran, and Nemuro were the four principal centers, and the first two led in the export of fish, much of it canned, to the rest of Japan. In normal times large quantities of canned crab and salmon also were shipped abroad.

Hokkaido's chief importance to Japan has been as a source of coal, timber, and wood pulp. Industrial activity was a secondary and less advanced development, but some 18 percent of the population were employed in manufacturing.

It has been estimated that Hokkaido contains some 40 percent of Japan's coal resources, production in 1936 being 9 million metric tons, or one-fifth of the total. Future prospects for the industry are more favorable here than in Kyushu, the leading island in the production of coal, as methods of extraction are more modern and mechanized and the cost per ton is lower. By 1944 it is estimated that about 10 million metric tons, or nearly one quarter of the total domestic output, was produced in Hokkaido, a surplus of 5 to 6 million metric tons being available for export from Otaru, Muroran, Kushiro, and Hakodate for use in industrial areas in Honshu. The most important coalfield lies in the east of the Ishikari Valley, running south from Fukagawa.

Two Fischer-Tropsch synthetic oil plants and two low-temperature carbonation plants have been set up in Hokkaido to utilize the abundant coal supplies. Hokkaido Jinzo Sekiyu operated the two large plants, at Rumoi and Takigawa in the west, while low-temperature carbonation plants were located at Iwamizawa and possibly also at Muroran. The combined output, if these plants were operated at full capacity, would be an important contribution to Japan's fuel-oil supply.

About 72 percent of Hokkaido is forested; the island produced 16 percent of Japan's timber and 40 percent of her wood pulp. There has been a tendency for production of the latter to increase in recent years and to overshadow the output of Karafuto. There are important pulp mills owned by the Oji Paper Company at Kushiro, Tomakomai, Ebetsu, Asahigawa, and Shokotsu.

The most important of the war industries in Hokkaido has been the iron and steel industry. Virtually the entire iron and steel capacity is concentrated in Muroran, representing 10 percent of Japan's domestic pig iron, and 4 percent of her steel-ingot capacity. Much of the pig iron and steel ingots are exported to Honshu, as rolling mill capacity in Hokkaido is relatively small. Imports of iron ore would be necessary if the plants were to operate at full capacity. The two largest operating firms, the Japan Iron and Steel Works and the Japan Steel Company, are located at Muroran. The Japan Iron and Steel Works is one of the major iron and steel plants in Japan, with a capacity of just under a million metric tons of pig iron and 293,000 metric tons of metallurgical coke. Together with the Japan Steel Works, some 600,000 metric tons of steel ingots and 200,000 metric tons of rolled products could be produced. The latter also manufactures tanks, naval ordnance, and armor plating.

Electric power generated in Hokkaido amounts to some 640,000 kilowatts, of which 400,000 kilowatts are supplied by hydro plants, the largest being at Nayoro, some 44 miles north of Asahigawa (65,000 kilowatts). The important industrial center of the Ishikari basin, with its coal mines, synthetic oil plants, and pulp mills, relies on three important steam plants for its power: the Shimizusawa (75,000 kilowatts), the Sunagawa (65,000 kilowatts), and the Ebetsu (50,000 kilowatts).

The main function of the railway system of Hokkaido is the transport of raw material resources to the ports, as shown by the fact that the only double-track trunk lines are from Yubari and Sunagawa in the Ishikari coalfield to the ports of Tomakomai and Otaru, respectively. There are four single-track lines of importance. One runs from Hakodate (the terminus of the railway ferry from Honshu) by way of Sapporo, Iwamizawa, Sunagawa, and Takigawa to Asahigawa, which is an important junction and the terminus of the second line, which runs to Wakkanai, the most northerly port and starting point of the railway ferry to Karafuto. The Nemuro line runs westward through Kushiro and Obihiro, and then northwest to Takigawa, thus providing a link between the two most important coal-mining and industrial regions on the island. The southern part of the Ishikari plain is connected by the fourth main line with Muroran. A branch line between Shimo-Furano and Asahigawa connects the first three main lines and encloses a triangular area between Asahigawa, Takigawa, and Shimo-Furano, which is the most densely populated region of Hokkaido. A second outstanding triangle is formed by the railway lines linking Sapporo, Iwamizawa, and Tomakomai. Probably one-half of all rail traffic on the island is concentrated in these two triangles.

Coastal movement of materials is a feature of Hokkaido transportation as well as of traffic to other Japanese islands. The chief ports are Hakodate, Muroran, Kushiro, Wakkanai, Otaru, and Nemuro, though the latter is closed by ice in winter. On the whole, the western and southern coasts are ice-free all the year round, as is the Soya Straits between Hokkaido and Karafuto.

Of all ports, Hakodate, Otaru, and Muroran have the largest cargo-handling capacities on Hokkaido, and their ranking among all Japanese ports is estimated at 9th, 10th, and 21st, respectively. Hakodate is the terminus of the rail ferry service to Aomori in Honshu. Eight or probably nine vessels, each above 3,500 G. R. T., were used in this service. Some, possibly 5, of these vessels had three parallel railway tracks capable of accommodating 20 to 25 freight cars; the others were used exclusively for freight traffic and could handle about 40 freight cars. Reports indicate that between 6 and 9 of these ferries were sunk or damaged in the mid-July carrier strikes.

The chief freight carried from Hokkaido by sea included coal, timber, fish, wood pulp, foodstuffs, iron, and steel. Trade is chiefly with Honshu, from which in normal times Hokkaido imported industrial equipment and general manufactured articles. Iron ore was imported from Korea and coking coal from Karafuto.

Hokkaido already produces essential materials in large quantities, but it is evident that the future potentialities of the island are very great. Agriculture is hampered by factors which have already been stated, but improved drainage in some of the less developed lowland areas and scientific seed selection could extend the area under cultivation and increase the range of crops, the yield, and the exportable surplus. Moreover, a growth in population and the development of power supplies might well lead to an advance in general manufacturing, while the coal and iron resources are capable of still further developments.

The Economic Importance of Manchuria

From an international point of view the economic importance of Manchuria has been mainly as a source of raw and semi-finished materials. These materials have been used for the last 14 years for the benefit of Japan's war economy. The reorientation of this economy toward China will be a delicate operation, and determination of the extent of Soviet economic influence in the area will be a question of first importance.

Manchuria is predominantly an agricultural region. The Central Lowlands, with their cold winters, hot summers, and sparse rainfall, have a natural grass vegetation. These grasslands were used for centuries by nomadic tribes who from time to time invaded the neighboring agricultural lands. The Manchus, who set up their dynasty in China in 1644, were the last invading force. The Manchu rulers kept Manchuria as a hunting preserve and restricted settlement in that area. However, as the pressure of population grew in China and as the Manchus became weaker, successive waves of immigrants from northern China settled on the fertile grasslands and substituted an agricultural for a grazing economy. With the complete breakdown of the Manchu rule in 1911, there were no more restrictions on such settlement.

The Japanese, who had obtained control of the South Manchurian railroad after the Russo-Japanese War, fostered this settlement, so that by 1940 there was a population of 43 million people in "Manchukuo," the puppet state set up in Manchuria by the Japanese. These agriculturalists grew wheat, corn, millet, kaoliang (grain sorghum), and soy beans. Some of these crops, especially soy beans, were for export.

Around the edges of the Central Lowlands are the forested mountain lands which provide timber for construction and other purposes in this area. There was some agricultural encroachment into these forested sections, particularly along the Korean border, where over a half million Koreans took up agricultural pursuits.

The Japanese, using the South Manchurian Railway Company, have been active for the last three decades in exploiting the mineral resources of Manchuria and in gaining control over the economic life of the region. With the establishment of the puppet state of "Manchukuo" in 1931 and 1932 this exploitation was turned toward the development of resources which would aid the Japanese war economy. In its broad aspects this development was aimed at the primary processing of raw materials and the encouragement of such industries as would provide for local needs. The coke, iron, and steel plants, centered at Anshan and Penhsihu in the Mukden area, were the heart of Manchurian heavy industry. Local raw materials were processed into steel, which was then exported to Japan, and, as local industries developed, also used in Manchuria. In order to meet the further requirements of the Japanese war economy, the hydroelectric power resources of Manchuria have been developed in the last decade. Large projects on the Yalu River and the headwaters of the Sungari River have been constructed and put into operation. Important uses of this power included the chemical, munitions, aluminum, and magnesium industries. In order to counter the lack of petroleum, the extensive shale-oil deposits at Fushun near Mukden were exploited.

During the last years of the war increasing emphasis was placed on the industrialization of Manchuria. This emphasis resulted in part from a growing shortage of shipping which forced the Japanese to reduce their imports of Manchurian raw materials in favor of processed goods, especially pig iron. However, the actual output and transfer of goods fell short of plans.[1] Further efforts to circumvent difficulties in shipping led to the development of double-track rail lines from northern China through Manchuria to Korea, terminating at the port of Fusan.

The economic future of Manchuria will depend to a large extent upon Chinese and Soviet policy. The resources of the land and people and the advanced industrial development will be of great aid to the postwar industrial growth of China. The agricultural resources will be of benefit to the U. S. S. R. The uprooting of Japanese economic control will be a necessary preliminary to the reorientation of Manchuria toward the economy of China.

[1] See "Intentions and Capabilities of the Japanese for Transferring Their Industrial War-making Potential to the Asiatic Mainland," *Weekly Summary*, Number 123 (17 May 1945), pp. 19–21.

BIBLIOGRAPHICAL NOTES

1. A well-arranged bibliography is The Intelligence Revolution: A Historical Perspective, Special Bibliography Series, No. 76, United States Air Force Academy Library, October, 1988.

2. John Foster Dulles' brother, Allen W. Dulles, was Director of the Central Intelligence Agency and wrote an interesting book; The Craft of Intelligence, Harper & Row, New York, 1963. A book on the family is by Leonard O. Mosley, Dulles: A Biography of Elinor, Allen and John Foster Dulles and Their Family Net-work, Dial Press, New York, 1978.

3. An account of the "Inquiry" is given in John Kirkland Wright, Geography in the Making, The American Geographical Society, 1851-1951, The American Geographical Society, New York, 1952, pages 199-202.

4. Many books on intelligence and covert operations discuss the Special Operations Executive. Three books are Edward Spiro, Inside S.O.E.; The Story of Special Operations in Western Europe, 1940-45, Barker, London, 1966; David Stafford, British and European Resistance, 1940-45; A Survey of the Special Operations Executive, With Documents, University of Toronto Press, Toronto, 1980; Charles Cruikshank, SOE in the Far East, Oxford University Press, New York, 1983.

5. The bibliography compiled by the Air Force Academy Library, op cit., has citations for many books on ULTRA and MAGIC. A useful bibliographical article is by Alexander S. Cochrane, Jr., " "MAGIC," "ULTRA," and the Second World War: Literature, Sources, and Outlook," Military Affairs, Vol. 46, pages 88-92, 1982. Some books are classics, such as David Kahn, The Codebreakers: The Story of Secret Writing, Macmillan, New York, 1967; Edward Van der Rhoer, Deadly MAGIC: A Personal Account of Communication Intelligence in World War II in the Pacific, Scribner, New York, 1978; Ronald Lewin, ULTRA Goes to War: The First Account of World War II's Greatest Secret, Based on Official Documents, McGraw-Hill, New

York, 1978; Ronald Lewin, The American MAGIC: Codes, Ciphers and the Defeat of Japan, Farrar Strauss, New York, 1982; and Edwin T. Layton, "And I Was There": Pearl Harbor and Midway--Breaking the Secrets, William Morrow, New York, 1985.

6. The air attack on the Japanese plane in which Admiral Yamamoto was flying is well described in John Costello, The Pacific War, 1941-1945, Rawson, Wade, New York, 1981, pages 401-403. A personal account of the intelligence aspect is in Edwin T. Layton, op. cit., pages 474-476.

7. There have been numerous conferences and symposia on the subject of British and American intelligence activities. An interesting collection of papers have been recently edited by K.C. Robertson, British and American Approaches to Intelligence, Macmillan Press, New York, 1987.

8. Many books on the Pacific War or on intelligence operations include discussions of the use of intelligence by the Japanese and by the Americans at the time of the attack on Pearl Harbor. The Congressional hearings in 1945-46, after the end of World War II, on Pearl Harbor were published in 39 volumes. One of the best analytical works is by Roberta Wohlstetter, Pearl Harbor, Warnings and Decisions, Stanford University Press, Stanford, California, 1962. A totally different, popular account is by Walter Lord, Day of Infamy, Henry Holt, New York, 1957. A few "revisionist" historians have inferred that Pearl Harbor was a plot by President Roosevelt to get the United States into World War II. Some of the revisionists books are listed in an article by Alvin D. Coox, "Repulsing the Pearl Harbor Revisionists: The State of Present Literature on the Debacle," Military History, January 1985, Vol. 49, pages 29-31. John Costello, op cit., has an interesting discussion of the newly available intelligence materials on Pearl Harbor in the last chapter of his book, pages 615-659.

9. The role of intelligence in the Battle of Midway is well described in Edwin T. Layton, op. cit.

10. There are a number of histories of the Battle of Okinawa. Two of the official histories have been reprinted. One stresses the United States Army actions: Roy E. Appleman, James M. Burns, Russell A. Gugeler and John Stevens, Okinawa, The Last Battle, Charles E. Tuttle Company, Rutland, Vermont, Tokyo, Japan, original date of

publication, 1948. The other stresses the actions of the United States Marine Corps: Chas. S. Nichols, Jr. and Henry I. Shaw, Jr., Okinawa, Victory in the Pacific, Charles E. Tuttle Company, Rutland, Vermont and Tokyo, Japan, original date of publication, 1955.

11. An excellent study of the collapse of Japan and the ending of the Pacific War is by Leon V. Sigal, Fighting to a Finish: The Politics of War Termination in the United States and Japan, 1945, Cornell University Press, Ithaca, New York, 1988. Professor Sigal notes in his preface that "In an era of nuclear weapons, when enormous and indiscriminate devastation can take place in a very short span of time, the problem of war termination assumes much greater significance than it held in earlier eras. . ."

12. The Weekly Summary of 2 August 1945 referred to the Potsdam Proclamation, though it would have been correct to refer to it as the Potsdam Declaration. Leon V. Sigal, op. cit., gives the interesting background on the shaping and promulgating of this Declaration.

13. The translation of the Japanese word: mokusatsu has been discussed in many of the books and articles on the surrender of Japan. Leon V. Sigal, op. cit., pages 147-153 is fair in his description of the linguistic nuance. An interesting article which drew attention to this was by Kazuo Kawai, "Mokusatsu, Japan's Response to the Potsdam Declaration," Pacific Historical Review, Vol. 19, November, 1950, pages 409-414. One of the early writers on the surrender is Robert J.C. Butow, Japan's Decision to Surrender, Stanford University Press, Stanford, California, 1854.

14. There are many books in Russian on the Soviet Union's entry and operations in the Pacific War. One of the most official has been translated into English: Finale, A Retrospective Review of Imperialist Japan's Defeat in 1945, Progress Publications, Moscow, 1972.

15. The estimates of the strength of the Kwantung Army available in 1945 gave it more ability than it had. There was a considerable amount of intelligence on the order of battle numbers and other characteristics of the Kwantung Army, but this intelligence was massive and there were no computers which could handle this data effectively at the time. This may be considered as an intelligence failure for though the data was available it was not analyzed sufficiently. The Japanese intelligence, also, was faulty in giving

accurate knowledge on the Soviet Armed Forces. This is well documented in an article by Edward J. Drea, "Missing Intentions: Japanese Intelligence and the Soviet Invasion of Manchuria, 1945," Military Affairs, April, 1984, Vol. 48, pages 66-73.

16. The radio broadcast of the Emperor of Japan has been given a great deal of attention recently, after the death of the Emperor. The recording of the broadcast in the Palace and the movement of the discs to the broadcasting studios were done with great caution, for fear of the attempts of die-hard Japanese Army fanatics to stifle the voice of the Emperor. John Costello, op. cit., gives an account of this and notes that "not once was the word "surrender" used in the Emperor's speech."

17. The Effects of Strategic Bombing on Japan's War Economy, Overall Economic Effects Division, The United States Strategic Bombing Survey, U.S. Government Printing Office, Washington, D.C. December 1946.

18. Philip Knightley, The Second Oldest Profession, Spies and Spying in the Twentieth Century, W.W. Norton, New York, 1987.

ABOUT THE AUTHOR

Shannon McCune was born in Sonch'on, Korea in 1913; his parents were Presbyterian missionaries. With a B.A. from the College of Wooster, an M.A. from Syracuse University and a Ph.D. in Geography from Clark University, he began teaching at Ohio State University in 1939.

During the Pacific War, as noted in this book, Shannon McCune was involved in economic intelligence activities for the Board of Economic Warfare and its successor agency, the Foreign Economic Administration. He served as the FEA representative on the Joint Intelligence Staff of the Joint Chiefs of Staff during the last six months of the war, writing and editing articles and notes for the Weekly Summary of the Joint Intelligence Committee. In recognition of his intelligence work in China in 1944 and 1945 he was awarded in 1946 a Presidential decoration, the Medal of Freedom.

In the decades after his war-time activities, Shannon McCune has served in many teaching, research and administrative positions in the United States and abroad. He has written a number of books and many articles and is listed in various biographical compendia. He is now Professor Emeritus of Geography and Asian Studies at the University of Florida, Gainesville, Florida.